500 RECIPES FOR VEGETABLES AND SALADS

MOYA MAYNARD

HAMLYN
LONDON · NEW YORK · SYDNEY · TORONTO

The author extends her thanks to the following for their
help and advice:

Danish Agricultural Producers
Hassy Perfection Celery
Danepak Limited
Olives from Spain
American Long Grain Rice
Hellmann's Real Mayonnaise
Mazola Pure Corn Oil
Marmite Information Service
British Sugar Bureau
McCormick Foods

Cover photograph by Paul Williams

Published by The Hamlyn Publishing Group Limited
London · New York · Sydney · Toronto
Astronaut House, Feltham, Middlesex, England

First published 1980
Fourth impression 1984

ISBN 0 600 39172 8

Printed and bound in Great Britain by R. J. Acford.

Contents

Introduction

I hope the users of this book will enjoy the recipes as much as I have enjoyed creating them.

The variety of dishes that can be made using vegetables and salads is endless, especially as there are always different vegetables coming into each season.

The more vegetable cooking one does the more the ideas come; the different combinations of flavour and texture help to make interesting dishes and one can go on indefinitely. I have kept mainly to the more usual vegetables, since these are more widely available.

Useful Facts and Figures

Notes on metrication

In this book quantities are given in metric and Imperial measures. Exact conversion from Imperial to metric measures does not usually give very convenient working quantities and so the metric measures have been rounded off in units of 25 grams. The table below shows the recommended equivalents.

Ounces	Approx. grams to nearest whole figure	Recommended conversion to nearest unit of 25
1	28	25
2	57	50
3	85	75
4	113	100
5	142	150
6	170	175
7	198	200
8	227	225
9	255	250
10	283	275
11	312	300
12	340	350
13	368	375
14	396	400
15	425	425
16 (1 lb)	454	450
17	482	475
18	510	500
19	539	550
20 (1¼ lb)	567	575

Note: When converting quantities over 20 oz first add the appropriate figures in the centre column, then adjust to the nearest unit of 25. As a general guide, 1 kg (1000 g) equals 2.2 lb or about 2 lb 3 oz. This method of conversion gives good results in nearly all cases, although in certain pastry and cake recipes a more accurate conversion is necessary to produce a balanced recipe.

Liquid measures: The millilitre has been used in this book and the following table gives a few examples.

Imperial	Approx. ml to nearest whole figure	Recommended ml
¼ pint	142	150
½ pint	283	300
¾ pint	425	450
1 pint	567	600
1½ pints	851	900
1¾ pints	992	1000 (1 litre)

Spoon measures: All spoon measures given in this book are level unless otherwise stated.

Can sizes: At present, cans are marked with the exact (usually to the nearest whole number) metric equivalent of the Imperial weight of the contents, so we have followed this practice when giving can sizes.

Oven temperatures

The table below gives recommended equivalents.

	°C	°F	Gas Mark
Very cool	110	225	$\frac{1}{4}$
	120	250	$\frac{1}{2}$
Cool	140	275	1
	150	300	2
Moderate	160	325	3
	180	350	4
Moderately hot	190	375	5
	200	400	6
Hot	220	425	7
	230	450	8
Very hot	240	475	9

An Imperial/American guide to solid and liquid measures

Solid measures

IMPERIAL	AMERICAN
1 lb butter or margarine	2 cups
1 lb flour	4 cups
1 lb granulated or castor sugar	2 cups
1 lb icing sugar	3 cups
8 oz rice	1 cup

Liquid measures

IMPERIAL	AMERICAN
$\frac{1}{4}$ pint liquid	$^2/_3$ cup liquid
$\frac{1}{2}$ pint	$1\frac{1}{4}$ cups
$\frac{3}{4}$ pint	2 cups
1 pint	$2\frac{1}{2}$ cups
$1\frac{1}{2}$ pints	$3\frac{3}{4}$ cups
2 pints	5 cups ($2\frac{1}{2}$ pints)

Note:
When making any of the recipes in this book, only follow one set of measures as they are not interchangeable.

Notes for American and Australian users

In America the 8-oz measuring cup is used. In Australia metric measures are now used in conjunction with the standard 250-ml measuring cup. The Imperial pint, used in Britain and Australia, is 20 fl oz, while the American pint is 16 fl oz. It is important to remember that the Australian tablespoon differs from both the British and American tablespoons; the table below gives a comparison. The British standard tablespoon, which has been used throughout this book, holds 17.7 ml, the American 14.2 ml, and the Australian 20 ml. A teaspoon holds approximately 5 ml in all three countries.

British	American	Australian
1 teaspoon	1 teaspoon	1 teaspoon
1 tablespoon	1 tablespoon	1 tablespoon
2 tablespoons	3 tablespoons	2 tablespoons
$3\frac{1}{2}$ tablespoons	4 tablespoons	3 tablespoons
4 tablespoons	5 tablespoons	$3\frac{1}{2}$ tablespoons

Vegetables - Introduction

Vegetables are so versatile that they can feature in almost any part of a meal. They can be used to make appetizing and often elegant starters. Homemade soups take a lot of beating both as starters and as light meals in themselves, and here there are a number of unusual and interesting ones.

The main course section makes full use of a wide range of vegetables and also includes pasta and pulse vegetables to give variety and to make economical and nourishing main dishes.

Serving vegetables as an accompaniment should add interest as well as colour and texture to a meal. For special occasions, when one can allow more time for preparation, it is worth trying more elaborate vegetable recipes for a change.

Use vegetables when in season and at their cheapest for freezing, salting and making pickles and chutneys, to preserve them for use throughout the year.

A-Z Vegetables

Basic preparation, cooking and serving

Artichokes-Globe

To prepare: Cut off stalks close to lower leaves. With scissors, snip points from leaves. Wash well in cold water and drain. Rub leaves with lemon to prevent discoloration. To remove choke, cut off top leaves, pull outside leaves away from the heart, scoop out choke (fine hairs) with a knife or spoon. This leaves the fond intact – often used stuffed as garnish. Keep in cold water with lemon juice added.

To cook: Boil: Whole, put head first into boiling salted water 40-45 minutes. The base will be tender when pricked with a fork or a base leaf pulls out easily. Without choke, boil 15-20 minutes. Drain upside down.

Steam: Whole, about 1 hour. Without choke: 20-25 minutes. May be braised, usually stuffed.

To serve: Either hot or cold on individual plates (1 per person) with melted butter or Hollandaise sauce or vinaigrette served separately. Leaves are pulled off with fingers and dipped into sauce. The fond or heart is the choice part and is cut into pieces to eat.

Artichokes-Jerusalem

To prepare: Scrub clean and peel after cooking or peel thinly under water. When peeled, keep in cold water with lemon added to retain colour.

To cook: Boil: Cover with cold water, salt and lemon juice added, 25-30 minutes until tender. Strain. Rub off skins if not peeled first.

Steam: 35-40 minutes.

Sauté: Blanch 5-10 minutes, drain and sauté in butter.

Roast: Blanch, cook in fat with meat or separately 40-50 minutes.

To serve: With melted butter, Hollandaise, Béchamel or cheese sauce.

Asparagus

To prepare: Cut off any woody part from base, scrape away white part from lower stem. Put all heads level and tie in bundles of 8-10 stems (1 average serving).

To cook: Stand bundles upright in a pan of boiling salted water to just below tips for 15-20 minutes. Tips are delicate and cook in the steam. Drain thoroughly protecting the tips. Pat dry on kitchen paper.

To serve: With melted butter or Hollandaise sauce.

Aubergines

To prepare: Trim off both ends, including leaves. Wipe clean. Cut, in half lengthwise to stuff, in slices or cubes. To make more tender, sprinkle cut surfaces with salt to draw out excess moisture. Leave on kitchen paper 30 minutes. Rinse and dry.

To cook: Fry: In oil and/or butter about 15 minutes. May first be coated with flour.
Grill: Brush with oil or melted butter, grill for 5-10 minutes. Turn during cooking.
Bake: Often stuffed, flesh scooped out, chopped and mixed with filling OR plain halved, brushed with oil about 40 minutes.

To serve: As accompaniment, stuffed as light meal or starter.

Avocado pears

To prepare: Use a stainless steel knife, cut in half lengthwise, twist halves to separate and remove stone. Coat cut surface with lemon juice to prevent discolouring.

To cook: Bake: In skins (sprinkled with seasoning and lemon) in hot oven about 10 minutes.

To serve: Fill baked avocado with hot savoury mixture.

Beans-broad

To prepare: Very young beans, wash, snip off ends, use whole or sliced. Shell mature beans.

To cook: Boil: In salted water 15-20 minutes, mature beans up to 30 minutes until tender. Strain.

To serve: Tossed in melted butter, with white or parsley sauce. Mature beans may be puréed with butter and herbs.

Beans-French

To prepare: Young beans, wash, snip off ends, use whole or cut in 3-cm/1½-inch lengths. Mature beans, remove string from sides.

To cook: Boil: In salted water 5-10 minutes. Drain.
Steam: About 20 minutes.

To serve: Toss in melted butter or top with flavoured butter.

Beans-runner

To prepare: As for French beans, cut slanting in 5-cm/2-inch lengths.

To cook: As for French beans.

To serve: Plain or tossed in butter or white parsley sauce.

Beetroot

To prepare: Cut off stalk leaving 5-cm/2-inch length. Wash carefully in cold water to avoid damaging skin and colour bleeding out.

To cook: Boil: Cover with cold water, boil 1-2 hours depending on size until just tender. Drain, rub off skins.
Steam: About 2 hours.
Bake: Wrapped in foil or brushed with oil, in moderate oven 45-60 minutes.

To serve: Small whole, sliced or cubed, tossed in butter, glazed or in piquant sauce.

Broccoli

To prepare: Remove rough outer leaves. Trim and scrape thick stems. Wash in cold water.

To cook: Boil: In salted boiling water 10-15 minutes. Test stems for tenderness. Drain carefully to protect spears.
Steam: 20 minutes.

To serve: With melted butter, Hollandaise or Bearnaise sauce.

Brussels sprouts

To prepare: Remove any outer discoloured leaves, cut off excess stalk. Cut cross into base of stalk. Wash in cold water.

To cook: Boil: In minimum boiling salted water 8-10 minutes. Drain.

To serve: Plain or tossed in melted butter.

Cabbage-green and white

To prepare: Remove coarse outer leaves. Cut into quarters. Cut out hard core. Wash well in cold water. May be shredded.

To cook: Boil: In boiling salted water, quarters 10-15 minutes, shredded 5-10 minutes. Drain.
Stuff separated leaves may be blanched, filled with stuffing and rolled. Usually braised.

To serve: Plain or tossed in melted butter. Stuffed as a main course.

Cabbage-red

To prepare: Cut out hard core and shred. Wash in cold water.

To cook: Braise: Boil in boiling salted water 2 minutes. Drain. Cook with little stock, vinegar and seasonings in covered pan or casserole on top or in moderate oven 1½-2 hours.

To serve: With cooking juices boiled to reduce.

Calabrese

To prepare: As for broccoli. Has white, green or purple spears.
To cook: As for broccoli.
To serve: As for broccoli or with cream sauce or buttered fried breadcrumbs.

Carrots

To prepare: Trim off both ends including stalk. Young carrots, scrub or scrape. Mature carrots, peel. Use small young carrots whole, mature cut in fingers, cubes, sticks or slices.
To cook: Boil: In salted water 10-20 minutes depending on size. Drain.
Steam: 20-25 minutes.
To serve: Plain, tossed in melted butter with herbs or in Béchamel sauce. May be puréed with butter.

Cauliflower

To prepare: Remove any outer damaged leaves. Retain fresh green leaves. Trim off excess stalk. Cut cross into base of stalk if cooking whole or separate into florets depending on size. Wash in cold water.
To cook: Boil: In minimum boiling salted water, whole up to 35 minutes depending on size, florets 10-15 minutes. Drain.
To serve: Whole or florets in white or cheese sauce.

Celeriac

To prepare: Wash well and leave whole or peel thickly and cut into slices, cubes or sticks.
To cook: Boil: In salted water with lemon juice, whole 50 minutes to 1 hour depending on size, pieces 20-25 minutes. Drain.
To serve: With melted butter, Hollandaise or Béchamel sauce.

Celery

To prepare: Cut off root end and leaves, cut stalks level. Wash and scrub clean in cold water. Use whole heart with some outer stalks removed or separate stalks and cut into 5-cm/2-inch lengths.
To cook: Boil: Pieces in boiling salted water or stock 15-20 minutes.
Braise: Hearts on bed of flavouring vegetables with stock in top of moderate oven 1-1½ hours.
To serve: Pieces with parsley or cheese sauce using part celery stalk in preparing. Braised hearts with cooking juices boiled to reduce.

Chard-seakale, beet

To prepare: Cut off any black roots and leaves from main ribs. Use leaves raw in salads or chop coarsely and cook separately. Wash well in cold water. Cut stalks in even lengths, tie in bundles like asparagus.
To cook: Boil: Stalks in salted water with lemon juice 15-20 minutes: should not be over cooked, just crisp. Drain.
Steam: 25-30 minutes.
Boil: Leaves in minimum salted water about 10 minutes. Drain well.
To serve: Stalks, with melted butter or Hollandaise sauce. Leaves, with butter.

Chicory

To prepare: Remove any damaged or limp leaves. Trim off stem, scoop out core. Wash in cold water.
To cook: Boil: In boiling salted water with lemon juice 25-30 minutes. Drain.
Braise: Blanch in boiling water, salted, for 5 minutes. Drain. Cook in little water or stock with lemon juice and butter 20-25 minutes.
To serve: Plain with chopped herbs or butter or white sauce.

Cos lettuce

To prepare: Remove any outer damaged leaves. Cut off stalk base. Wash well in cold water and drain. Leaves may be separated and shredded.
To cook: Boil: Leaves in salted water for 10 minutes. Drain.
Braise: Whole about 30 minutes.
Sauté: Shredded leaves in butter 2-3 minutes.
To serve: Boiled with Mornay or Hollandaise sauce. Sautéed as accompaniment Chinese style.

Courgettes

To prepare: Trim both ends. Wash in cold water. Use whole or slice thickly or cut in half lengthwise to stuff.
To cook: Boil: Sliced in boiling salted water 4-5 minutes; whole 10-15 minutes depending on size.
Steam: Whole 6-8 minutes.
Sauté: Slices in butter 5-10 minutes.
To serve: Tossed in butter with chopped herbs.

Endive-curly

To prepare: Discard any tough outside leaves. Trim stalk base. Wash well in cold water. Drain.
To cook: Boil: In boiling salted water about 20 minutes. Drain.
To serve: Plain or tossed in melted butter.

Fennel

To prepare: Trim root and stalk end. Scrub well in cold water. Use whole or slice thinly. Keep leaves for garnish or to flavour sauce.

To cook: Boil: Whole in boiling salted water or stock 30-40 minutes depending on size.

Sauté: Slices. First blanch whole in salt water. Drain well. Slice and sauté in butter about 10 minutes turning during cooking to colour.

To serve: Whole fennel cut in slices, tossed in melted butter garnished with fennel leaves.

Kale

To prepare: Cut stems and thicker ribs from leaves. Cut into pieces. Wash well in cold water.

To cook: Boil: In boiling salted water 10-15 minutes. Drain well.

To serve: Tossed in melted butter or with Béchamel sauce.

Leeks

To prepare: Cut off roots and green tops leaving about 8-cm/3-inches intact. Wash several times in cold water to remove grit. Use whole or cut in thick slices.

To cook: Boil: In salted water 10-15 minutes. Drain well.

Braise: First blanch in boiling salted water 4-5 minutes. Drain. Braise on bed of vegetables, flavourings and little stock about 50 minutes.

To serve: Tossed in melted butter or with Béchamel sauce. Braised with juices boiled to reduce.

Mange tout peas

To prepare: Trim both ends and remove side strings. Wash in cold water and drain.

To cook: Boil: In boiling salted water 4-5 minutes. Drain well.

Sauté: In butter 5-10 minutes.

To serve: Boiled plain or tossed in melted butter with chopped fresh herbs.

Marrows

To prepare: Slice thickly, peel and remove seeds. May be cut into cubes. Or wash skin, halve lengthwise or slice off a "lid", scoop out seeds ready for stuffing.

To cook: Steam: Rings or pieces 20-30 minutes depending on size.

Sauté: In butter in covered pan about 10 minutes.

Stuff: With savoury mixture, wrap in foil or cover and bake in moderate oven about 2 hours.

To serve: Steamed, in white sauce or with fresh herbs.

Mushrooms

To prepare: Trim base of stalks. Cultivated mushrooms, wipe with damp cloth. Field mushrooms,

peel, wash and drain well. Use whole, or quarter, slice or chop.

To cook: Boil: In little boiling water with lemon juice and seasoning 2-3 minutes.

Sauté: In butter with lemon and seasoning 4-5 minutes.

To serve: With cooking juices, fresh chopped herbs or cream boiled with juices.

Onions-British

To prepare: Cut off stalk end, peel off thin outer skin. If using whole, cut off a little of the root end. Slice in thin or thick rings. To chop, cut onion in half through stalk and root ends. Hold between thumb and finger, slice at intervals in same direction. Put flat side down, slice through one way, turn onion and slice other way making small dice. To chop very finely, make these cuts close together, chop dice more if necessary.

To cook: Boil: In salted water, whole 30-40 minutes. Drain well.

Sauté or fry: Slices or chopped in oil or butter 10-15 minutes until soft and browned.

Deep fry: Dip slices in milk and flour, deep fat fry 3-4 minutes.

Braise: Whole onions on bed of flavouring vegetables, seasonings and little stock on top or in moderate oven 30-40 minutes.

Roast: Blanch 2-3 minutes, cook in fat around joint or separately 30-40 minutes.

To serve: Whole, boiled or sautéed slices in Béchamel or cheese sauce or glaze whole boiled in butter. Braised may be separate dish. To accompany or as part of a main dish.

Onions-Spanish

To prepare: Trim root end and some green leaf, leaving about 8-cm/3-inches intact. Remove any discoloured outer skin. Wash in cold water. May be chopped.

To cook: Sauté: In butter about 5 minutes until lightly brown and still crisp.

To serve: In sauce or part of a dish.

To braise: Blanch, cook in salted water 15 minutes, drain. Place in buttered dish, pour over melted butter, sprinkle with castor sugar, salt and pepper and a little brown stock. Cook in moderate oven until nicely browned.

Parsnips

To prepare: Trim both ends, removing stalk. Peel. Use young parsnips whole, mature parsnips cut into fingers slices or cubes. Remove core if tough.

To cook: Boil: In salted water, whole 30-40 minutes depending on size.

Sauté: Blanch 2-3 minutes. Drain. Sauté in butter 10-15 minutes.

Deep fry: Fingers or slices, blanch 4-5 minutes. Drain. Dip in batter, deep fat fry 3-4 minutes.
Roast: Blanch 2-3 minutes, drain. Roast in fat around the joint or separately 30-40 minutes.
Steam: Small young parsnips 30 minutes, slices 15 minutes.
To serve: Boiled, tossed in melted butter with chopped fresh herbs as accompaniment. Purée boiled parsnips with butter and seasoning.

Peas

To prepare: Shell, discard any damaged peas. Wash in cold water. Drain.
To cook: Boil: In boiling salted water with mint and little sugar 10-15 minutes. Drain, discard mint.
Braise: With other vegetables, butter and little stock on top or in moderate oven 20-30 minutes, depending on age of peas.
To serve: Boiled, tossed in melted butter with fresh chopped herbs. Braised with flavouring vegetables and little juice. As accompaniment.

Peppers-red and green
(Capsicum)

To prepare: Cut off stalk end. Use whole for stuffing, cut out membrane, remove seeds. Or halve and de-seed, cut in slices or cubes. Wash in cold water. Drain. May be grilled or baked whole until skins darken, then peeled.
To cook: Sauté: Slices, cubes in butter or oil 10-15 minutes.
Stuff: Blanch 2-3 minutes. Stuff, brush with oil, bake in moderate oven 30-40 minutes.
To serve: Baked stuffed as a main course. Sautéed as accompaniment or part of a dish.

Potatoes

To prepare: New, wash in cold water. Skins may be scraped off. Old, scrub in cold water or peel. Cut large potatoes to even sizes.
To cook: Boil: In skins or peeled in boiling salted water 15-20 minutes depending on size. Drain. Return to pan without lid on low heat, allowing steam to escape and make potatoes floury.
Steam: In skins about 1 hour.
Roast: Blanch 2-3 minutes. Drain. Roast in fat around joint or separately, about 45 minutes depending on size. Baste with fat during cooking.
Sauté: Boil whole or large pieces in salt water 15 minutes until just tender. Drain and dry out over heat. Slice and brown both sides in butter or oil.
Bake: Jacket (in skins). Use even sizes. May be wrapped in foil or rubbed with oil and salt. Bake in fairly hot oven about 1 hour depending on size.
Deep fry: Peeled potatoes cut in $\frac{1}{2}$-1-cm/$\frac{1}{4}$-$\frac{1}{2}$-inch thick slices, then in $\frac{1}{2}$-1-cm/$\frac{1}{4}$-$\frac{1}{2}$-inch chips. Soak in

cold water 20 minutes to remove loose starch. Drain and dry thoroughly. Deep fat fry 190°C, 325°F, 7-8 minutes. Lift out in basket, reheat fat, return chips for 2-3 minutes until brown and crisp. Drain on kitchen paper.
Game chips: Slice on gauffrete or single grater soak in cold water, drain and fry for 5-6 minutes.
Straw potatoes: Slice in very fine matchsticks, soak, dry and fry 5-6 minutes.
To serve: Boiled, peeled or in skins, topped with butter and fresh chopped herbs. Baked, jacket, cross cut into top of potato; squeeze from the base to loosen flesh, put a butter-pat into the opening. All potatoes as accompaniment. Also part of a dish. Mashed: boiled potatoes mashed to purée with butter and seasoning.

Potatoes-sweet

To prepare: Scrub clean in cold water. Cut in pieces if large. May be peeled and sliced.
To cook: Boil: In skins in salted water 15-20 minutes depending on size. Drain, return pan without lid to low heat allowing steam to escape.
Steam: about 1 hour.
Sauté: Peeled and sliced, blanch 2 minutes. Drain well. Sauté in butter until tender and brown on both sides.
Bake: In skins, in fairly hot oven about 1 hour depending on size.
Deep fry: Peeled, sliced potatoes. Soak in cold water, drain and dry. Deep fat fry 5-10 minutes. Drain on kitchen paper.
To serve: Boiled and steamed, peeled or in skins, plain or tossed in butter. Mashed to purée with butter and seasoning. Baked, in skins, cross cut into top of potato, squeezed open, butter and seasoning put into opening. As accompaniment or part of a dish.

Radishes

To prepare: Trim root and stalk ends. Wash in cold water. Drain.
To cook: Boil: Whole in salted water 5-10 minutes. Drain.
Sauté: Blanch 1-2 minutes, drain, sauté in butter about 5 minutes.
To serve: Whole in parsley or cream sauce.

Salsify

To prepare: Trim root and stalk ends. Scrub clean or peel. Cut in pieces about 5-cm/2-inches length. Put in cold water with lemon to prevent discolouring.
To cook: Boil: In salted water with lemon juice 25-30 minutes. Drain. Peel if necessary.
To serve: Tossed in melted butter or with white or Bearnaise sauce.

Seakale

To prepare: Trim stalks, cut in even lengths. Wash in cold water. May be tied in bundles like asparagus.
To cook: Boil: In salted water with lemon juice 15-20 minutes. Drain well.
Steam: 20-25 minutes.
To serve: With melted butter, Hollandaise, Bearnaise, Béchamel or cheese sauce.

Shallots

To prepare: Trim both ends. Remove skin. Soaking in boiling water 1-2 minutes helps to loosen skins. Use whole, slice or chop.
To cook: Boil: Whole in stock or water 10-15 minutes. Drain.
Sauté: Boiled whole in butter 5-10 minutes. Add sugar to glaze and chopped fresh herbs.
To serve: Boiled in cream sauce or glazed.

Spinach

To prepare: Remove stalk and coarse ribs. Wash several times in cold water to remove grit. Drain.
To cook: Boil: Coarser leaves in minimum boiling salted water 5-10 minutes. Drain well. Young spinach in water clinging to leaves and butter in uncovered pan 5-10 minutes. Drain if necessary.
To serve: Tossed in melted butter. Chopped or sieved to purée with butter, cream and seasonings, usually nutmeg.

Spring cabbage

To prepare: Remove stalk and coarse ribs. Slice or shred. Wash in cold water. Drain.
To cook: Boil: In minimum boiling salted water 5-10 minutes. Drain well.
Steam: 10-15 minutes.
To serve: Plain or tossed in melted butter. Vinegar or herbs may be added.

Swedes

To prepare: Trim root and stalk ends. Peel thickly. Use small swede whole. Cut in pieces, slices, fingers or cubes.
To cook: Boil: In salted water 15-20 minutes depending on size.
Steam: 20-30 minutes.
Roast: Blanch 2 minutes. Drain. Roast in fat around joint or separately 1-1¼ hours depending on size.
To serve: Plain or tossed in butter. Add chopped fresh herbs. Mashed to purée with butter and seasonings.

Sweetcorn

To prepare: Cut off stalk, remove husks and silk. To separate kernels from cob, stand on one end, with sharp knife cut downwards, turn cob on to other end and repeat. Wash in cold water. Drain.
To cook: Boil: In salted water, on cob 10-15 minutes depending on size. Kernels should come off easily. Kernels, cook in minimum boiling salted water for 5-10 minutes. Drain.
Bake: Wrapped in foil with butter, seasonings, in fairly hot oven 30-40 minutes depending on size.
To serve: Whole on cobs, with corn holders piercing each end of stalk. In special corn dish with melted butter and seasoning. Kernels, tossed in melted butter or with well-seasoned sauce.

Tomatoes

To prepare: Remove stalk. Wipe clean. To remove skin, cover with boiling water for 2 minutes, put into cold water and skin or hold tomato on a fork in flame, rotating until skin chars and bursts. Use whole, cut a cross in smooth end, or halved, quartered or in thick slices. For stuffing, slice "lid" from smooth end, scoop out seeds and stand upside down to drain.
To cook: Fry: Halved, quartered or sliced in butter or oil 3-4 minutes.
Grill: Halved, topped with seasoning, sugar, butter 3-4 minutes.
Bake: Whole or halved, brush with oil and bake in moderate oven 20-25 minutes. May be stuffed with savoury filling and baked.
To serve: As accompaniment; stuffed as separate course as a starter.

Turnips

To prepare: Trim root and stalk ends. Young turnip scrub clean. Mature turnip, peel thickly. Cut in pieces, slices, fingers or cubes.
To cook: Boil: Whole in skins or peeled in salted water 20-30 minutes depending on size. Drain. Rub off skins.
Steam: Large pieces 15 minutes.
To serve: Mashed to purée with butter, cream seasonings. Whole, peeled in various sauces. Slices, fingers, cubes, plain with fresh chopped herbs or tossed in butter.

Watercress

To prepare: Break off thick stalks, remove any wilted leaves. Wash in cold water. Drain. May be chopped.
To cook: Sauté: Blanch in boiling salted water 1 minute. Drain well, sauté in butter 5 minutes.
To serve: In soups, sauces, fillings. As accompaniment.

Pressure Cooking Vegetables

Choose vegetables for pressure cooking carefully because age and freshness as well as the size of the pieces will affect the length of cooking time. Experience will help to determine the exact times.

Cook all the following vegetables at high pressure in water brought to the boil before cooking to help green vegetables retain colour. Follow manufacturer's booklet for amount of liquid to use. Immediately reduce temperature under cold water to prevent over-cooking.

Asparagus

To prepare: Wash, trim and tie into bundles of 4-6 spears. Place on trivet.
To cook: 2-4 minutes, depending on thickness.
To serve: As a starter, hot with melted butter or Hollandaise sauce, cold with vinaigrette.

Beetroot

To prepare: Cut off tops, leaving a little stem. Peel after cooking.
To cook: a) Small beetroots. Allow 600 ml/1 pint water and cook 10 minutes.
b) Medium beetroots. Allow 900 ml/1½ pints water and cook for 15-20 minutes.
c) Large beetroots. Allow 1200 ml/2 pints water and cook for 25-30 minutes.
To serve: Either hot with Béchamel sauce or cold with vinegar.

Broad beans

To prepare: Shell and place in separator.
To cook: 4-5 minutes.
To serve: With parsley sauce.

Broccoli

To prepare: Trim and divide into spears. Place in a separator.
To cook: 3-4 minutes.
To serve: With melted butter sprinkled with nutmeg or ground black pepper.

Brussels sprouts

To prepare: Trim and cut a cross in the base of each. Place in separator.

To cook: 3-4 minutes.
To serve: With cooked chestnuts, melted butter or sprinkled with grated nutmeg.

Cabbage

To prepare: Trim, discard stalk and shred. Place in separator.
To cook: 3 minutes.
To serve: With melted butter or a few caraway seeds.

Carrots

To prepare: Peel, slice or cut into sticks. Young ones may be left whole. Place in separator or on the trivet.
To cook: 3-4 minutes.
To serve: With melted butter and chopped parsley or Béchamel sauce.

Cauliflower

To prepare: Trim and divide into sprigs. Place on the trivet.
To cook: 3-4 minutes. Whole – 5-8 minutes.
To serve: With Béchamel sauce as a vegetable or cheese sauce for a light meal.

Celery

To prepare: Trim and cut into 5-cm/2-inch lengths. Place in separator or on trivet.
To cook: 3-4 minutes.
To serve: With Béchamel sauce or melted butter and black pepper.

Celeriac

To prepare: Peel and cube, or cut into 2.5-cm/1-inch sticks. Cover with cold water until ready to place in separator.
To cook: 3 minutes.
To serve: With parsley or mashed with butter and pepper.

Chicory

To prepare: Discard any loose outer leaves. Place whole on trivet, dot with butter and sprinkle with lemon juice.
To cook: 3-6 minutes.
To serve: With Béchamel or cheese sauce.

Corn on the cob

To prepare: Remove leaves and silks. Place whole on trivet.
To cook: Small – 3 minutes.
Large – 5 minutes.
To serve: With ground black pepper and melted butter.

Courgettes

To prepare: Slice. Place in separator.
To cook: 3 minutes.
To serve: With melted butter and black pepper.

Fennel

To prepare: Trim, discard leafy tops and halve. Place on trivet.
To cook: 3-6 minutes.
To serve: With cheese sauce.

French beans

To prepare: Top, tail and place on trivet.
To cook: 3 minutes.
To serve: With melted butter or cold in a salad.

Globe artichokes

To prepare: Remove outer leaves. Place on trivet.
To cook: Small – 6 minutes.
Large – 10 minutes.
To serve: With melted butter or French dressing.

Jerusalem artichokes

To prepare: Peel. Place on trivet.
To cook: 4-5 minutes.
To serve: With Béchamel sauce and black pepper.

Leeks

To prepare: Trim and slice. Wash well. Place in separator.
To cook: 2-3 minutes.
To serve: With Béchamel sauce or melted butter.

Marrows

To prepare: Skin, slice thickly and discard seeds. Place on trivet.
To cook: 4 minutes.
To serve: With Béchamel or cheese sauce or melted butter.

Onions

To prepare: Peel and slice. Place in separator. Peel, leave whole and place on trivet.
To cook: Sliced – 4 minutes.
Whole – 6-8 minutes.
To serve: With Béchamel sauce or melted butter.

Parsnips

To prepare: Peel and cube. Place in separator or on trivet.
To cook: 3-4 minutes.
To serve: Whole or mashed with butter and black pepper.

Peas

To prepare: Shell. Place in separator with a sprig of mint.
To cook: 3-4 minutes.
To serve: With melted butter or cold in a salad.

Potatoes (new)

To prepare: Scrape and leave whole. Place in separator or on trivet.
To cook: 4-5 minutes.
To serve: With melted butter and chopped parsley or chives.

Potatoes (old)

To prepare: Peel and quarter. Place in separator or on trivet.
To cook: 3-4 minutes.
To serve: Creamed with butter and hot milk; with a knob of butter and chopped parsley.

Runner beans

To prepare: String and slice. Place in separator.
To cook: 4 minutes.
To serve: With a knob of butter or cold in a salad.

Swedes

To prepare: Peel and cube. Place in separator.
To cook: 4 minutes.
To serve: Mashed with butter and black pepper.

Turnips

To prepare: Peel and slice. Place in separator. Young, whole, place on trivet or in separator.
To cook: Sliced – 3-4 minutes.
Whole – 3-4 minutes.
To serve: Sliced – mashed with butter.
Whole – with melted butter and black pepper.

Starters

Chilled avocado mousse

You will need for 6 servings:

METRIC/IMPERIAL

150 ml/¼ pint milk
slice of onion
blade of mace
1 small bay leaf
3 large ripe avocado
  pears
4 teaspoons lemon
  juice

15 g/½ oz butter
1 tablespoon plain
  flour
2 teaspoons gelatine
seasoning
1 egg white

1 Infuse the milk with the onion, mace, bay leaf, heat gently and remove from the heat; leave on one side for about 20 minutes.
2 Halve the avocados, cover one half with cling film.
3 Remove stones and skin from the remaining halves, sieve or liquidize the flesh.
4 Mix with 3 teaspoons of the lemon juice.
5 Melt the butter, add the flour, cook for 1 minute, strain the milk and gradually add to the flour.
6 Bring to the boil, stirring, and cook for 2 minutes, then cool slightly.
7 Dissolve the gelatine in 3 tablespoons of very hot water.
8 Season the avocado and add to the sauce with the dissolved gelatine.
9 Whisk the egg white until stiff and fold into the mixture.
10 Turn into 6 individual soufflé dishes. Put in a cool place to set.
11 Slice the remaining avocado halves, dip into the remaining lemon juice and use to garnish the top of each dish.

Avocados sevilliana

You will need for 4 servings:

METRIC/IMPERIAL

1 teaspoon Dijon
  mustard
1 teaspoon castor
  sugar
2 teaspoons cider
  vinegar
150 ml/¼ pint double
  cream

75 g/3 oz prawns,
  shelled
75 g/3 oz stuffed
  green olives
seasoning
2 large avocados
little lemon juice

1 Mix together the mustard, sugar and vinegar.
2 Whip cream until stiff. Stir in mustard mixture.
3 Reserve 4 prawns and 4 olives for garnish.
4 Slice remaining olives and stir into cream with prawns and seasoning.
5 Cover and leave to stand for 30 minutes in a cool place.

6 Cut avocados in half, remove stones and brush flesh with lemon juice.
7 Place on serving dishes, and fill centres with the prawn and olive dressing.
8 Garnish each with a prawn and an olive and serve chilled.
Variation:
Instead of the mustard add ½ teaspoon concentrated curry sauce to the cream.

Avocado and egg pâté

You will need for 4 servings:

METRIC/IMPERIAL

1 ripe avocado pear
juice of ½ lemon
2 hard-boiled eggs
100 g/4 oz cottage
  cheese
1 clove garlic, crushed
2 tablespoons double
  cream

1 teaspoon chopped
  chives
seasoning
4 crisp lettuce leaves
to garnish:
4 slices lemon
sprigs of parsley

1 Halve the avocado pear, remove the stone and scoop out all the flesh. Toss in the lemon juice and mash until smooth.
2 Sieve the hard-boiled eggs and cottage cheese, then mix with the avocado and garlic.
3 Stir in the cream and chives; taste and season. (Alternatively, liquidise the avocado, lemon, eggs, cottage cheese and garlic together until smooth then stir in the cream and chives. Season to taste.)
4 Serve piled on crisp lettuce leaves. Garnish with slices of lemon and sprigs of parsley.
Variation:
Use a low fat cream cheese instead of sieving the cottage cheese and finely mash the egg.

Artichokes vinaigrette

You will need for 4 servings:

METRIC/IMPERIAL

4 globe artichokes
salt
lemon juice

French dressing (see
  page 86)

1 Cut off the stems of the artichokes close to the leaves and cut approximately 2 cm/1 inch off the tops of each.
2 Trim remainder of the leaves with scissors.
3 Place in a pan of boiling salted water with some lemon juice and simmer the artichokes for 30 minutes until the bottoms are tender.
4 Drain and refresh in cold water.

5 Remove the centres of each artichoke with a sharp knife and carefully scrape away all the 'choke' leaving four clean 'shells'.

6 Serve with French dressing.

Variations:

1 Serve hot with melted butter.

2 Serve cold: Fill with Hollandaise sauce (see page 85), garnish with anchovy fillets.

Artichoke cream

You will need for 4 servings:

METRIC/IMPERIAL

225 g/8 oz Jerusalem artichokes	½ teaspoon grated nutmeg
1 teaspoon lemon juice	¼ teaspoon mustard salt
75 g/3 oz curd cheese	grated nutmeg
150 ml/¼ pint double cream	

1 Scrub the artichokes thoroughly and trim.

2 Cook in boiling salted water for approximately 5-10 minutes until just tender but not broken up. Cool slightly and remove skins.

3 Liquidise the artichokes with the lemon juice, curd cheese and 2 tablespoons of the double cream.

4 Add the nutmeg and mustard to the artichokes and season lightly with the salt.

5 Whip the remaining cream and fold in, then chill thoroughly.

6 Serve in individual dishes, sprinkled lightly with grated nutmeg.

7 Hot buttered toast or slices of pumpernickel should be served with this cream.

Variation:

Make half the above quantity and use to fill 2 ripe, halved and stoned avocado pears. Sprinkle with grated nutmeg before serving.

Aubergines with yoghurt sauce

You will need for 4 servings:

METRIC/IMPERIAL

2 medium-sized aubergines	2 teaspoons chopped chives
salt	1 (150-g/5.3-oz) carton natural yoghurt
little flour	
freshly ground black pepper	2 tablespoons mayonnaise (see page 87)
1 egg, beaten	to garnish:
100 g/4 oz fresh white breadcrumbs	sprigs of watercress
oil for frying	tomato wedges

1 Wash the aubergines and slice. Sprinkle with salt and leave to stand for 30 minutes. Drain, rinse and dry well.

2 Season the flour with pepper. Dip the aubergine slices into the flour then the egg and coat in breadcrumbs.

3 Heat the oil in a frying pan and fry the aubergines for a few minutes on either side until crisp and golden. Drain on kitchen paper.

4 Mix together the chives, yoghurt and mayonnaise. Season with pepper and serve with the aubergines.

5 Garnish the slices with sprigs of watercress and wedges of tomato.

Ratatouille

You will need for 6 servings:

METRIC/IMPERIAL

3 tablespoons olive oil	350 g/12 oz courgettes
1 medium-sized Spanish onion, sliced	3 tablespoons water
	1 teaspoon dried oregano
1 clove garlic, halved	½ teaspoon castor sugar
350 g/12 oz aubergines	2 large tomatoes
1 medium red pepper	

1 In a large saucepan, place the oil with the onion and garlic and cook gently without browning for 10 minutes.

2 Meanwhile, prepare the vegetables. Wash and trim the aubergine and cut into 2-cm/1-inch chunks.

3 Wash the pepper, remove the seeds and cut into 2-cm/1-inch pieces.

4 Wash and trim courgettes and cut into 2-cm/1-inch pieces.

5 Add these prepared vegetables to the saucepan and stir round carefully.

6 Add the water, oregano and sugar.

7 Cover and bring to the boil, then reduce heat to medium and cook for about 30 minutes, stirring occasionally.

8 Cut the tomatoes in wedges, add to the saucepan and just heat through.

9 Serve either hot or cold.

Variations:

1 Using half the quantity, add freshly chopped basil as an alternative to dried oregano.

2 Dried marjoram could be used instead of oregano.

3 More tomatoes could be used and a green pepper instead of red.

4 Freshly ground pepper is a nice addition.

Asparagus and ham pancakes

You will need for 4 servings:

METRIC/IMPERIAL

300 ml/½ pint pancake batter (see page 38)	40 g/1½ oz butter
	25 g/1 oz flour
8 slices lean ham	150 ml/¼ pint milk
24 fresh thick asparagus spears, cooked and drained	3 tablespoons thin cream
	2 tablespoons grated cheese

1 Make 8 thin pancakes in a 20-cm/8-inch frying pan.
2 Place a slice of ham on each pancake and three asparagus spears on each piece of ham. Roll up pancakes to enclose filling. Place in a flameproof dish.
3 Melt butter over low heat in another pan. Remove pan from heat and stir in flour to make a roux. Gradually stir in milk and cream, beat until smooth. Cook for 2 minutes.
4 Pour sauce over the pancakes and sprinkle with grated cheese.
5 Heat gently under a moderate grill for about 10 minutes or until cheese is bubbling.

Stuffed aubergines

You will need for 4 servings:
METRIC/IMPERIAL

2 large aubergines of a good shape (approx. 350 g/12 oz each)	½ teaspoon dried oregano
4 tablespoons oil	pinch dried thyme
1 medium onion, chopped	seasoning
100 g/4 oz streaky bacon	2 tomatoes
1 clove garlic, crushed	25 g/1 oz grated Parmesan cheese
75 g/3 oz fresh breadcrumbs	*to garnish:* parsley

1 Wash the aubergines and trim off the ends.
2 Cut in half horizontally.
3 Scoop out the flesh using a spoon, to within 0.5 cm/¼ inch of the walls.
4 Chop the flesh and leave on one side.
5 Heat the oil in a frying pan and fry the aubergines outside down for about half a minute.
6 Drain and place in an ovenproof dish skin side down. Keep on one side.
7 Fry the onion until beginning to brown.
8 Remove rind from the bacon and chop, add to the onion with the garlic.
9 Cook for a minute, then add the aubergine flesh. Cook for about 10 minutes stirring occasionally.
10 Mix the breadcrumbs, herbs and seasoning together in a bowl.
11 Remove the fried mixture from the pan with a slotted spoon and leave any extra liquid in the pan.
12 Mix into the breadcrumbs, etc. and pile into the aubergines.
13 Slice the tomatoes, arrange them between the aubergines and sprinkle with the cheese.
14 Cover with foil and cook in a moderate oven (180°C, 350°F, Gas Mark 4) for 45 minutes to 1 hour until the aubergines are tender.
15 Serve either hot or cold, garnished with parsley.
Variations:
1 Use minced beef, lamb or veal instead of the bacon.
2 Use prawns to make a seafood filling, in addition to or instead of the bacon.

Courgettes paysanne

You will need for 4 servings:
METRIC/IMPERIAL

1 medium onion	1 teaspoon dried marjoram
450 g/1 lb courgettes	seasoning
50 g/2 oz butter	50 g/2 oz grated cheese
1 (398 g/14 oz) can peeled tomatoes	

1 Prepare onion and slice thinly.
2 Wash courgettes, trim off the ends and cut courgettes into 1-cm/½-inch slices.
3 Melt the butter in a large saucepan.
4 Add all the ingredients except the cheese.
5 Cover and simmer gently for 20-25 minutes, turning frequently until the courgettes are just tender.
6 Turn the mixture into an ovenproof dish.
7 Sprinkle the top with the grated cheese.
8 Place under a preheated grill for about 5 minutes to melt and lightly brown the cheese.

Broccoli au gratin

You will need for 6 servings:
METRIC/IMPERIAL

450 g/1 lb broccoli	225 g/8 oz tomatoes
6 slices shoulder ham	1 teaspoon Marmite
50 g/2 oz Cheddar cheese, grated	seasoning
for the sauce:	pinch sugar
1 tablespoon corn oil	1 tablespoon tomato purée
100 g/4 oz onions, chopped	

1 To make the sauce, place oil and onions in a small saucepan and cook for 5 minutes.
2 Add the roughly-chopped tomatoes and cook until mushy, about 10 minutes.
3 Stir in the Marmite, seasoning, sugar and tomato purée.
4 Trim and cook the broccoli in boiling salted water until just tender, 10-15 minutes depending on thickness.
5 Divide broccoli between the ham slices and roll up.
6 Place in an ovenproof dish.
7 Spoon the sauce over the broccoli and sprinkle with cheese.
8 Place the dish under a moderate grill to reheat the broccoli and just melt the cheese.

Celery cheese mousse

You will need for 8 servings:
METRIC/IMPERIAL

25 g/1 oz gelatine	6 stuffed olives, chopped
75 ml/2½ fl oz water	1 dessert apple, grated
225 g/8 oz Danish blue cheese, grated	300 ml/½ pint yoghurt or mayonnaise (see page 87)
3 sticks celery, finely chopped	seasoning
1 medium green pepper, finely chopped	*to garnish:* apple slices and celery leaves
1 small onion, minced or finely chopped	

1 Dissolve the gelatine in the water in a small bowl over a gentle heat and leave to cool.
2 Mash the cheese with a fork and add the celery, pepper, onion, olives and apple.
3 Stir in the yoghurt or mayonnaise and mix thoroughly. Season to taste.
4 Stir in the cooled gelatine and transfer the mixture to a wetted 1-litre/2-pint ring mould. Chill until firm. Turn out and decorate with celery leaves and apple slices.
5 Serve either as a starter or buffet snack with a tossed salami and rice salad.

Variation:
Spoon into individual ramekins and decorate each with a slice of hard-boiled egg.

Celery hearts à la grecque

You will need for 8 servings:

METRIC/IMPERIAL	
4 celery hearts	pinch salt
juice of 2 lemons	300 ml/½ pint thick
600 ml/1 pint water	mayonnaise (see
150 ml/¼ pint olive oil	page 87)
1 bay leaf	2-3 tablespoons wine
12 peppercorns	or herb vinegar
12 coriander seeds	16 anchovy fillets
	8 black olives

1 Cut the celery hearts (trim off the leaves) in half and wash in cold water.
2 Place the lemon juice, water, oil, herbs and seasonings in a pan and bring to the boil.
3 Place the celery halves in it and poach covered until tender, approximately 20 minutes, depending on size. Drain well and cool.
4 When completely cold arrange the halves on a serving dish.
5 Mix together the mayonnaise and vinegar and coat each of the halves. Decorate each with 2 anchovy fillets and a black olive.

Variation:
Use wine vinegar and add some freshly chopped herbs to the mayonnaise.

Savoury herbed mushrooms

You will need for 6 servings:

METRIC/IMPERIAL	
for the dressing:	¼ teaspoon garlic salt
1 (142-ml/5-fl oz)	or salt and pepper
carton soured	1 tablespoon fresh
cream	dill, chopped
2 teaspoons tomato	225 g/8 oz button
ketchup	mushrooms,
2 tablespoons	washed
mayonnaise	
1 tablespoon French	
dressing (see page	
86)	

1 Mix the dressing ingredients together.
2 Halve the mushrooms where necessary and toss in the dressing.
3 Chill in refrigerator for 1 hour before serving.

Variation:
Use ½ teaspoon dried basil.

Angela's mushrooms

You will need for 6 servings:

METRIC/IMPERIAL	
450 g/1 lb medium-	1 teaspoon French
sized open	mustard
mushrooms	1 tablespoon capers,
2 large eggs	chopped
seasoning	to garnish:
100 g/4 oz fresh	chopped parsley
breadcrumbs	bunch watercress
oil for frying	
for the sour cream	
sauce:	
1 (142-ml/5-fl oz)	
carton soured	
cream	

1 Wash the mushrooms, trim the stalks a little if necessary.
2 Break the eggs into a bowl, add 1 teaspoon water, beat well, and season.
3 Place crumbs in a bowl.
4 Dip the mushrooms into the egg and then coat with the crumbs.
5 Continue until all are crumbed.
6 Heat the oil and fry the mushrooms a few at a time until they are crisp on both sides. Keep hot and fry remainder.
7 To make the sauce, place soured cream in a bowl and beat in the French mustard, seasoning and capers.
8 Place sauce in a bowl, sprinkle with parsley. Place in the centre of a dish and arrange the mushrooms around with sprigs of watercress.

Variations:
1 Omit capers from the sauce and add crisply fried bacon crumbled into the sauce.
2 Omit capers and add a few chopped olives to the sauce.

Vegetable and nut pâté

You will need for 4 servings:

METRIC/IMPERIAL	
1 small onion	¼ teaspoon dried
2 sticks celery	marjoram
1 tablespoon oil	seasoning
2 tomatoes, skinned	2 eggs
1 small carrot	2 bay leaves
1 small parsnip	to garnish:
50 g/2 oz brown bread	lettuce
50 g/2 oz peanuts	tomato wedges
¼ teaspoon grated	
nutmeg	

1 Prepare and chop onion and celery. Fry in the oil until soft about 10 minutes.
2 Cut the tomatoes into quarters, remove the seeds.
3 Peel carrot and parsnip and cut up coarsely.
4 Mince the vegetables and tomatoes with the peanuts and bread.
5 Place in a bowl, add the seasonings and eggs well beaten.
6 Mix well and place in a ½-kg/1-lb loaf tin.
7 Arrange the bay leaves on top, cover with greased paper.
8 Stand tin in a roasting tin with about 2 cm/1 inch water.
9 Cook in a moderate oven (180°C, 350°F, Gas Mark 4) for about 1 hour.
10 When cold turn out and serve garnished with the salad ingredients.

Spinach-stuffed eggs

You will need for 6 servings:

METRIC/IMPERIAL

6 large eggs	Parmesan cheese
225 g/8 oz fresh spinach	seasoning
100 g/4 oz cream cheese	grated nutmeg
2 tablespoons grated	1½ tablespoons mayonnaise (see page 87)

1 Cover eggs with cold water, bring to the boil stirring gently to keep the yolks centred, cook for 10 minutes. Drain and crack; cover with cold water.
2 Wash the spinach well, remove tough stalks and place in a pan with the water that adheres to the leaves.
3 Cook gently until tender, stirring occasionally.
4 Drain well, then sieve it into a basin.
5 Cut the eggs in half lengthwise and scoop out the yolks and push through a sieve onto the spinach.
6 Add the remaining ingredients and mix well together until smooth. Taste and adjust seasoning.
7 Spoon or pipe the filling into the eggs.

Variation:
Use soured cream or cream instead of mayonnaise.

Flamenco eggs

You will need for 2 servings:

METRIC/IMPERIAL

2 tomatoes	little butter
4 stuffed green olives	seasoning
1 red pepper	2 eggs
50 g/2 oz button mushrooms	

1 Peel and slice the tomatoes. Slice the olives, pepper and mushrooms and mix with the tomatoes.
2 Divide between two individual ovenproof dishes. Dot with butter and season.
3 Bake in a moderately hot oven (200°C, 400°F, Gas Mark 6) for 10 minutes.

4 Crack an egg into the centre of each dish and bake for a further 4-5 minutes until set.
5 Serve at once.

Spinach eggs

You will need for 4 servings:

METRIC/IMPERIAL

2 (227-g/8-oz) packets frozen chopped spinach	100 g/4 oz dry white breadcrumbs
	fat for deep frying
100 g/4 oz fresh white breadcrumbs	for the sauce:
	15 g/½ oz butter
50 g/2 oz grated cheese	15 g/½ oz flour
	300 ml/½ pint milk
2 eggs, beaten	50 g/2 oz grated cheese
seasoning	
2 hard-boiled eggs	nutmeg
to coat:	to garnish:
2 eggs, beaten	tomato wedges

1 Cook the spinach according to the directions on the packet and drain thoroughly. Cool.
2 Mix together the breadcrumbs, cheese, beaten eggs and spinach. Season.
3 Using floured hands, coat the hard-boiled eggs with the spinach mixture. Dip in the beaten eggs and coat in breadcrumbs.
4 Deep fry until golden brown, drain on kitchen paper and keep warm.
5 To make the sauce melt the butter in a saucepan. Add the flour and cook, stirring continuously, for a few minutes. Stir in the milk and bring to the boil, then stir in the cheese and season.
6 Cook gently until the cheese has completely melted then add a generous pinch of nutmeg.
7 Cut the spinach eggs in half and arrange on a warmed serving dish. Pour over the sauce, sprinkle with a little nutmeg and garnish with tomato wedges.

Variations:
1 The spinach mixture may be formed into croquettes, coated with egg and breadcrumbs and shallow fried. Serve with the same sauce.
2 The hard-boiled eggs may be chopped and added to the spinach mixture and made into croquettes.

Antipasta party

You will need for 14-16 servings:

METRIC/IMPERIAL

250 ml/8 fl oz water	2 green peppers, diced
250 ml/8 fl oz olive oil	
1 bay leaf	2 red peppers, diced
few sprigs fresh thyme	1 head broccoli, washed and cut into small florets
2 cloves garlic, peeled	
seasoning	75 g/3 oz green olives
125 ml/4 fl oz white wine vinegar	75 g/3 oz black olives
	225 g/8 oz small button onions
½ head celery, washed and diced	
	225 g/8 oz button mushrooms
1 small cauliflower, washed and cut into small florets	225 g/8 oz small carrots, peeled

1 Place the oil, water, bay leaf, thyme, garlic, seasoning and white wine vinegar in a large saucepan.
2 Put in the prepared vegetables, leaving the olives, onions, mushrooms and carrots whole.
3 Bring to the boil, cover and simmer for 2-3 minutes until the vegetables are blanched but still crisp and hard. (They will soften when left in the marinade.) Place either in a large jar or bowl to cool until ready to use.
5 Serve with Soured cream sauce or Blue cheese sauce (see pages 87-8), and warm crusty wholemeal bread.

Variation:
Serve sprinkled with chopped parsley, chives or extra fresh herbs and a plain mayonnaise sauce.

Note:
This should be made 24 hours in advance. If more convenient, divide the vegetables between smaller jars, cover in the usual way as for chutneys and pickles. Keep up to 3 months only.

Whole beetroot salad

You will need for 4 servings:
METRIC/IMPERIAL
8 small round cooked beetroots
100 g/4 oz cottage cheese
1 tablespoon chopped fresh chives
2 tablespoons French dressing (see page 86)

seasoning
Worcestershire sauce
to garnish:
punnet of cress
chives (optional)

1 Remove skin from each beetroot, wash and dry on kitchen paper.
2 Scoop out the centre from each beetroot using a grapefruit knife or teaspoon, being careful not to break the flesh.
3 Chop the scooped out flesh.
4 Mix this with the cottage cheese, chives, dressing, seasonings and a dash of Worcestershire sauce.
5 Divide mixture between the beetroots.
6 Wash and drain the cress, arrange on a dish with the beetroots on top.
7 A few long chives coming out of the centre of each is an added garnish.

Variations:
1 Use ½ teaspoon of horseradish sauce in the filling, omitting the Worcestershire sauce.
2 A few toasted slivered almonds would also be a good garnish and give a bit of texture.

Grape and grapefruit salad

You will need for 4 servings:
METRIC/IMPERIAL
100 g/4 oz black grapes
2 large grapefruit
4 tablespoons French

dressing (see page 86)
1 tablespoon chopped parsley

1 Wash and halve the grapes, remove the pips.
2 Place the fruit in a small mixing bowl.
3 Halve the grapefruit. Carefully cut out the segments with a grapefruit knife, avoiding the white pith.
4 Place the grapefruit in the bowl with the grapes.
5 Pour the dressing over the fruit and leave to stand for 1 hour, stirring occasionally.
6 Return the fruit to the grapefruit shells or serve in individual glasses.
7 Serve sprinkled with the chopped parsley.

Variation:
Use pink grapefruit and green grapes.

Moya's celeriac salad

You will need for 4 servings:
METRIC/IMPERIAL
225 g/8 oz celeriac
1 tablespoon white malt vinegar
2 medium-sized carrots
pinch each salt, pepper, dry mustard and castor sugar

4 tablespoons corn oil
2 tablespoons white wine vinegar
few lettuce leaves

1 Wash and peel the celeriac, grate coarsely.
2 Put into a pan of cold water with the white malt vinegar and bring to the boil.
3 Strain the celeriac through a nylon strainer and allow to cool.
4 Peel and grate the carrots fairly finely.
5 Place the seasonings in a bowl, blend in the oil gradually, beat in the vinegar.
6 Mix the celeriac and carrot together, pour over the dressing and toss lightly.
7 Serve on individual dishes and garnish with a lettuce leaf.

Variations:
1 Add chopped parsley to the salad.
2 Use half quantity dressing and add to 3 tablespoons soured cream.

Cold celery and prawn starter

You will need for 6 servings:
METRIC/IMPERIAL
6 sticks celery
100 g/4 oz white button mushrooms, washed
1½ teaspoons paprika
1½ teaspoons curry powder
olive oil
2 tablespoons lemon juice

seasoning
175 g/6 oz peeled prawns
2 tablespoons chopped parsley
to garnish:
lemon wedges

1 Wash the celery sticks and cut into 1-cm/½-inch lengths. Place in a bowl.

2 Slice the mushrooms, including the stalks, thinly and mix with the celery.

3 Mix the paprika and curry powder with the olive oil.

4 Add the lemon juice and seasoning, then the prawns and chopped parsley.

5 Combine well with the celery and mushroom slices and transfer to a serving dish.

6 Chill before serving and garnish with wedges of lemon.

Variation:

Toss in a light mayonnaise (see page 87) but add 2 tablespoons single cream.

Celery and mushroom starter

You will need for 4 servings:

METRIC/IMPERIAL

8 sticks celery, washed and chopped	40 g/1½ oz butter or margarine
salt	2 tomatoes, skinned and chopped
½ bay leaf	grated rind of 1 lemon
juice of 1 lemon	chopped parsley
100 g/4 oz button mushrooms, washed and sliced	chopped chives (optional)

1 Simmer the celery gently in boiling salted water with the bay leaf and lemon juice.

2 Sauté the mushrooms lightly in the butter or margarine, then add the tomatoes and heat through.

3 Drain the celery well and add to the mushrooms and tomato.

4 Pile onto serving dish and sprinkle with the lemon rind, parsley and chives if used. Serve slightly chilled.

Vegetarian niçoise salad

You will need for 4 servings:

METRIC/IMPERIAL

4 hard-boiled eggs, cooled	2 tablespoons single cream
4 sticks celery, finely chopped	seasoning
¼ cucumber, peeled and finely chopped	3 tomatoes, skinned, seeded and coarsely chopped
300 ml/½ pint mayonnaise (see page 87)	to garnish: black olives chopped parsley

1 Cut eggs in half lengthways.

2 Mix together celery and cucumber and place most of them in bottom of salad bowl or serving dish.

3 Arrange egg halves on top, yolk side down, and sprinkle remaining cucumber and celery round them.

4 Mix together mayonnaise and cream, season to taste and coat the egg halves with it.

5 Place the chopped tomatoes in a line down centre of dish. Garnish with black olives, sprinkle with parsley and serve.

Variations:

1 Use stuffed olives instead of black or use some of each.

2 Shredded Webbs lettuce and salted peanuts would also be nice with the celery and cucumber.

3 Shredded Chinese cabbage leaves could be used instead of celery.

4 Use shredded lettuce, sliced potato, green beans and red peppers in layers in the base of a dish and top with the tomatoes, etc.

Guacamole dip with crudités

You will need for 6-8 servings:

METRIC/IMPERIAL

2 ripe avocado pears	1 tablespoon chopped parsley
juice of 1 lemon	2 tablespoons olive oil
1 clove garlic, crushed (optional)	seasoning
4 small tomatoes, peeled, seeded and chopped	for the crudités:
	3 sticks celery
1 small onion, peeled and finely chopped	1 red pepper, seeded
	1 green pepper, seeded
2 sticks celery, finely chopped	4 carrots, peeled
	1 small head fennel

1 Peel avocados and remove stones. Mash finely with a fork and mix with lemon juice, garlic, if used, tomatoes, onion, celery, parsley, oil and seasoning to taste.

2 Place in refrigerator to chill before serving.

3 Prepare the crudités and cut into sticks 7 cm/3 inches long and quite thin.

4 Serve the guacamole in a small dish in the centre of a plate, arrange the crudités round the edge.

Spanish dip

You will need for 6 servings:

METRIC/IMPERIAL

75 g/3 oz stuffed olives	1 tablespoon lemon juice
1 (99-g/3½-oz) can tuna steak, drained	1 tablespoon brandy
2 tablespoons capers, drained	pinch dry mustard
	225 ml/8 fl oz thick mayonnaise (see page 87)
5 anchovy fillets	
3 tablespoons oil	

1 Place the olives, tuna, capers, anchovy fillets, oil, lemon juice, brandy and mustard in a blender to give a thick purée.

2 Mix into the mayonnaise, taste and adjust seasonings.

3 Serve with crudités (see above).

Soups

Golden summer soup

You will need for 6-8 servings:

METRIC/IMPERIAL

1 large onion, chopped	1 litre/1¾ pints water
25 g/1 oz butter or margarine	strip of lemon peel
100 g/4 oz carrots	few sprigs fresh thyme
225 g/8 oz potatoes	2 stock cubes
225 g/8 oz fresh apricots	blade of mace
225 g/8 oz fresh tomatoes	1 bay leaf
	seasoning

1 Place the onion and butter or margarine in a saucepan, cook gently without browning until soft, about 10 minutes.
2 Peel and chop carrots and potatoes.
3 Halve apricots and remove stones.
4 Cut tomatoes into quarters.
5 Place these and remaining ingredients in a saucepan.
6 Bring to the boil, cover and simmer gently for 1 hour.
7 Sieve or liquidise the soup and reheat before serving.

Fresh vegetable soup

You will need for 4 servings:

METRIC/IMPERIAL

1 large onion, peeled and chopped	1.2 litres/2 pints white stock
3 carrots, peeled and sliced	pinch thyme
1 leek, chopped	few parsley stalks
225 g/8 oz potatoes, peeled and chopped	½ bay leaf
½ head celery, chopped	seasoning
50 g/2 oz butter	*to garnish:*
50 g/2 oz plain flour	chopped parsley or fried croûtons

1 Fry all the prepared vegetables in the melted butter for several minutes until softened but not coloured.
2 Stir in the flour and cook for a further 1-2 minutes.
3 Gradually blend in the stock, bring to the boil stirring and cook for 2 minutes.
4 Add the herbs and seasoning and cook for 30-45 minutes.
5 Remove bay leaf and serve very hot, garnished with chopped parsley; alternatively liquidise until smooth and garnish with fried croûtons.

Cream of artichoke soup

You will need for 4 servings:

METRIC/IMPERIAL

1 small onion	seasoning
25 g/1 oz butter or margarine	300 ml/½ pint milk
450 g/1 lb Jerusalem artichokes	*to garnish:*
300 ml/½ pint chicken stock	3 tablespoons single cream
	chopped parsley

1 Prepare and slice onion.
2 Melt the butter or margarine in a medium sized saucepan, add the onion and cook gently for 5 minutes without browning.
3 Meanwhile, peel the artichokes, slice thickly and add to the pan.
4 Cook for about 10 minutes, stirring, then add the stock, cook for a further 15 minutes until tender and season.
5 Sieve or liquidise.
6 Add the milk, reheat, add the cream and just before serving adjust seasoning to taste.
7 Serve sprinkled with the chopped parsley.

Asparagus soup

You will need for 6 servings:

METRIC/IMPERIAL

750 g/1½ lb fresh asparagus	2 strips of lemon peel
1 small onion	seasoning
15 g/½ oz butter or margarine	150 ml/¼ pint single cream
900 ml/1½ pints chicken stock	

1 Trim the asparagus, see notes on preparation (page 6). Cut the tips off.
2 Cook the tips in boiling salted water for 10-15 minutes depending on thickness until just tender. Drain and keep on one side.
3 Cut the remaining asparagus stalks into 2-cm/1-inch lengths.
4 Peel and finely chop the onion.
5 Melt the butter or margarine in a large saucepan and cook onion gently for 5 minutes without browning.
6 Add the stock, lemon peel and asparagus stalks.
7 Cover and simmer gently for about 20 minutes until the asparagus is tender.
8 Remove lemon peel, sieve or liquidise to give a purée.
9 Season the soup, reheat with the asparagus tips.
10 Add the cream, continue to heat and then serve.

Beetroot soup

You will need for 4-6 servings:

METRIC/IMPERIAL
1 large carrot	1 bay leaf
1 medium onion	1 tablespoon red wine
100 g/4 oz cabbage	vinegar
25 g/1 oz butter or	2 teaspoons castor
margarine	sugar
450 g/1 lb cooked	seasoning
beetroot	
1 litre/1¾ pints	
vegetable stock	

1 Peel the carrot and onion and grate finely.
2 Remove coarse leaves of the cabbage as they could make the soup bitter.
3 Remove hard stem and shred cabbage finely, but keep lengths short.
4 Melt butter or margarine in a large pan, add carrot, onion and the cabbage.
5 Cover the pan, cook very gently for 10 minutes, shaking occasionally.
6 Skin and grate the beetroot, add to the pan with the stock.
7 Add remaining ingredients, cover and simmer for about 20 minutes.
8 Taste soup and adjust seasoning.

Variations:

1 Sieve or liquidise the soup and serve with a swirl of cream or soured cream on top, sprinkled with a few chives.
2 Add some grated orange rind to the soup.

Cream of broccoli soup

You will need for 6 servings:

METRIC/IMPERIAL
450 g/1 lb fresh	2 teaspoons grated
broccoli	onion
600 ml/1 pint chicken	25 g/1 oz flour
stock	600 ml/1 pint milk
25 g/1 oz margarine or	150 ml/¼ pint single
butter	cream
	seasoning

1 Trim the broccoli if necessary and wash well.
2 Bring the chicken stock to the boil, add the broccoli and cook for 10-15 minutes until tender. The time will depend on the thickness of the stem.
3 Sieve or liquidise; keep on one side.
4 Melt the margarine or butter in a fairly large saucepan, add the onion and sauté until soft but not brown.
5 Add the flour and cook for 2 minutes.
6 Gradually stir in the milk to make a smooth sauce, bring to the boil and simmer for 3-4 minutes.
7 Add the broccoli purée to the sauce, heat through and then add the cream.
8 Taste and adjust seasoning.

Variation:

A cream of spinach soup could be made in the same way using a packet of frozen spinach and cooking it in 300 ml/½ pint chicken stock for the time stated on the packet. Then continue with the same quantities as for the cream of broccoli soup.

Cream of celery soup

You will need for 4 servings:

METRIC/IMPERIAL
600 ml/1 pint chicken	25 g/1 oz plain flour
stock	300 ml/½ pint milk
1 large head celery	celery salt
40 g/1½ oz butter or	pepper
margarine	
2 teaspoons grated	
onion	

1 Bring the stock to the boil in a large saucepan.
2 Wash and trim the celery and cut into 1-cm/½-inch lengths.
3 Place the celery in the boiling stock, cover and simmer for about 20 minutes until tender, longer if the celery is on the old side.
4 When cooked, sieve or liquidise.
5 Melt the butter or margarine, add the onion and cook for a few minutes.
6 Stir in the flour and cook for 2 minutes.
7 Gradually blend in the milk and bring to the boil, stirring. Cook for 2 minutes.
8 Add the celery liquor gradually. Add celery salt and pepper to taste.
9 Reheat gently and serve with a few chopped celery leaves on the top.

Variations:

1 Replace the milk with half milk and half single cream.
2 Use celery seed instead of the celery salt and season with salt and pepper.

Autumn celery and leek soup

You will need for 6-8 servings:

METRIC/IMPERIAL
½ head celery, sliced	½ lemon, juice and rind
450 g/1 lb leeks,	½ teaspoon dried basil
washed and sliced	½ teaspoon dried
1 clove garlic, crushed	oregano
with salt	½ teaspoon cumin
600 ml/1 pint tomato	seeds
juice	seasoning
1 tablespoon	1 teaspoon sugar
Worcestershire	1 bay leaf
sauce	

1 Place all the ingredients in a saucepan and cover.
2 Simmer for 20 minutes.
3 Check seasoning and reheat for 8 minutes.

Variation:

Cook in chicken stock, omit the basil, sieve or liquidise and serve with a little cream.

Celery and prawn soup

You will need for 6 servings:
METRIC/IMPERIAL
2 heads celery
50 g/2 oz butter
225 g/8 oz potatoes, peeled and sliced
1.2 litres/2 pints vegetable stock (or water and vegetable stock cube)
seasoning
225 g/8 oz peeled prawns
little cream (optional)

1 Trim and wash the celery very thoroughly. Chop finely.
2 Melt the butter in a large saucepan, add the celery and cook gently for 5 minutes.
3 Add the potatoes, stock and seasoning.
4 Bring slowly to the boil, reduce heat and simmer for 30 minutes.
5 Sieve or liquidise the soup.
6 Return the soup to a clean pan, stir in the prawns, reheat gently and serve at once, with a swirl of cream in each dish if used.

Cucumber and lemon soup

You will need for 4 servings:
METRIC/IMPERIAL
1 onion
15 g/½ oz butter
600 ml/1 pint chicken stock
2 lemons
1 cucumber
few sprigs lemon balm (optional)
1 teaspoon castor sugar
seasoning
150 ml/¼ pint single cream

1 Peel and chop the onion.
2 Melt the butter in a saucepan, add the onion and cook over a gentle heat until soft but not browned.
3 Add the chicken stock and grated rind and juice of the lemons.
4 Thinly peel about half of the skin from the cucumber and chop the cucumber roughly.
5 Add to the soup, with the sprigs of lemon balm if used. Bring to the boil, then cover and simmer for 20 minutes.
6 Sieve or liquidise the soup, add the sugar and season to taste.
7 Serve either hot or chilled with a little cream poured into the centre of each bowl.
Variation:
Omit the lemons, lemon balm and sugar from the soup. Add a few sprigs of mint with the cucumber and remove these before liquidising the soup. Add 150 ml/¼ pint milk to the soup and serve, either hot or cold, with the cream stirred in and garnished with a few sprigs of mint.

Mushroom soup

You will need for 4 servings:
METRIC/IMPERIAL
50 g/2 oz margarine
225 g/8 oz onions, chopped
225 g/8 oz mushrooms, chopped
¼ teaspoon dried basil
1 clove garlic, crushed
25 g/1 oz flour
2 teaspoons Marmite
300 ml/½ pint milk
seasoning
4 tablespoons single cream
to serve:
garlic croûtons or chopped parsley

1 Melt margarine, add onions, mushrooms, basil and garlic, cover and cook gently for 10 minutes, until onions are soft but not browned.
2 Stir in flour and cook for 2 minutes.
3 Dissolve 2 teaspoons Marmite in 600 ml/1 pint boiling water and gradually stir into onions, etc.
4 Bring to the boil, stirring, reduce heat and simmer for 15 minutes.
5 Remove from heat, stir in the milk and seasoning. Either sieve or liquidise. Add cream.
6 Reheat, adjust seasoning and serve with garlic croûtons or sprinkle with chopped parsley.

French onion soup

You will need for 6 servings:
METRIC/IMPERIAL
450 g/1 lb onions, sliced
25 g/1 oz margarine
2 tablespoons oil
1½ tablespoons Marmite
1 litre/1¾ pints water
25 g/1 oz flour
seasoning
to serve:
25 g/1 oz margarine
1 teaspoon Marmite
6 thin slices French bread
40 g/1½ oz Gruyère cheese, grated

1 Place the onions, margarine and oil in a saucepan, cover and cook gently for 15 minutes without browning.
2 Stir in the Marmite and ¾ litre/1½ pints water; simmer gently for 30 minutes.
3 Meanwhile, blend the flour with the remaining water.
4 Blend the margarine and Marmite together and lightly spread on each side of the French bread.
5 Place on a baking sheet and sprinkle each with the grated cheese.
6 Bake in a preheated oven (190°C, 375°F, Gas Mark 5) on the top shelf for 10 minutes to just melt the cheese.
7 Add the blended flour and water to the soup, stirring. Bring to the boil and cook for 5 minutes. Add seasoning to taste.
8 To serve, place a piece of French bread into 6 individual soup bowls and pour the soup over.

Watercress and tomato soup

You will need for 4-6 servings:

METRIC/IMPERIAL

4 rashers streaky bacon	2 tablespoons tomato purée
1 onion	150 ml/¼ pint milk
25 g/1 oz butter	seasoning
450 g/1 lb tomatoes	*to garnish:*
2 bunches watercress	sprigs of watercress
1 tablespoon flour	
600 ml/1 pint chicken stock	

1 Remove the rind from the bacon and chop.
2 Peel the onion and chop.
3 Melt the butter in a saucepan, add the bacon and onion and cook gently, stirring occasionally until soft but not browned.
4 Meanwhile, skin the tomatoes by blanching for a few seconds in boiling water.
5 Remove the stalks from the watercress.
6 Stir the flour into the bacon and onion then gradually add the stock, tomato purée, tomatoes and watercress.
7 Bring to the boil then cover and simmer for 15 minutes.
8 Sieve or liquidise the soup and stir in the milk.
9 Reheat gently, taste and season, then serve garnished with sprigs of watercress.

Cream of navet

You will need for 4-6 servings:

METRIC/IMPERIAL

450 g/1 lb turnips	seasoning
1 small onion	1 egg yolk
40 g/1½ oz butter	150 ml/¼ pint double cream
1 bay leaf	
600 ml/1 pint milk	*to garnish:*
300 ml/½ pint water	chopped parsley

1 Peel and thinly slice the turnips and onion.
2 Melt the butter in a medium saucepan, add the vegetables. Stir round, cover with a piece of buttered greaseproof paper.
3 Cover with the lid and cook very slowly for about 10-15 minutes until the vegetables are soft but not coloured.
4 Add the bay leaf, milk, water and seasoning.
5 Bring to the boil, reduce heat and cook very gently for 15 minutes.
6 Remove bay leaf and either sieve or liquidise the soup.
7 Rinse out the saucepan and return the soup to the pan.
8 Blend the egg yolk and cream together, add to the soup and reheat very gently otherwise the egg could curdle. Taste and adjust seasonings.
9 Serve at once with a little chopped parsley in each dish.

Variations:
1 A pinch of nutmeg may be added.

2 Serve with fried croûtons.
3 A little grated lemon rind mixed with the parsley would add extra colour.

Refreshing summer soup

You will need for 4 servings:

METRIC/IMPERIAL

600 ml/1 pint apple juice	5-cm/2-inch length cucumber
2 (142-ml/5-fl oz) cartons soured cream	½ small green pepper
	1 bunch watercress
300 ml/½ pint tomato juice	1 tablespoon cider vinegar
2 tablespoons finely chopped chives	seasoning

1 Blend the apple juice, soured cream and tomato juice together.
2 Stir in the chives.
3 Peel the cucumber and cut into small dice. Add to the soup.
4 Cut the green pepper into very thin slices, and add.
5 Wash and finely chop the watercress. Add this to the soup.
6 Add the vinegar and seasoning.
7 Chill well before serving. Taste and adjust seasonings if necessary.

Salad soup

You will need for 4 servings:

METRIC/IMPERIAL

2 small avocado pears	100 g/4 oz tomatoes, skinned and chopped
450 ml/¾ pint chicken stock	
1 (150-g/5.3-oz) carton natural yoghurt	5-cm/2-inch length cucumber, grated
	seasoning
2 teaspoons chopped chives	squeeze of lemon juice (optional)
150 ml/¼ pint tomato juice	

1 Halve the avocados, remove stones and peel off the skin, cut flesh into dice.
2 Sieve or liquidise the avocados using some of the stock to make it easier.
3 Mix remaining ingredients with the avocado. Add seasoning and extra stock if liked.

Cold avocado soup

You will need for 4-6 servings:

METRIC/IMPERIAL

10-cm/4-inch length cucumber	2 (150-g/5.3-oz) cartons natural yoghurt
600 ml/1 pint chicken stock	seasoning
2 ripe avocados	*to garnish:*
1 teaspoon lemon juice	chopped chives

1 Cut the cucumber into dice and cook in the stock, bring to the boil and simmer for 10 minutes. Allow to cool a little.
2 Halve the avocados, remove stones and skin. Sieve or liquidise with the cooked cucumber.
3 Add the remaining ingredients, cover and chill well before serving.
4 Sprinkle with chopped chives.

Cold cucumber soup

You will need for 4 servings:
METRIC/IMPERIAL
1 small onion
300 ml/½ pint chicken stock
1 small bay leaf
1½ cucumbers
1 (150-g/5.3-oz) carton natural yoghurt
150 ml/¼ pint milk
seasoning
chopped chives

1 Prepare and slice onion, place in saucepan with the stock and bay leaf.
2 Bring to the boil, cover and simmer.
3 Peel the cucumbers thinly, reserving a quarter.
4 Slice the cucumber and add to the stock.
5 Cover and simmer for 15 minutes.
6 Remove the bay leaf.
7 Sieve or liquidise the soup.
8 Leave to become cold.
9 Whisk in the yoghurt and milk.
10 Add seasoning to taste.
11 Serve with the remaining cucumber finely diced in the centre of each dish.
12 Sprinkle with the chopped chives.
Variation:
Add only the milk to the soup; stir the yoghurt and serve a spoonful in the centre of each dish.

Summer tomato soup

You will need for 4-6 servings:
METRIC/IMPERIAL
1 kg/2 lb tomatoes
1 tablespoon sugar
2 teaspoons salt
½ teaspoon onion juice or 1 teaspoon chopped chives
finely grated rind and juice of ½ lemon
4 thin slices ham
8-cm/3-inch length cucumber, peeled
150 ml/¼ pint single cream

1 Chop the tomatoes roughly.
2 Place the tomatoes in a pan and cook for about 10 minutes to give a purée, then sieve or liquidise. If liquidised, strain to remove skins.
3 Pour into a container and chill well.
4 Just before serving add the sugar, salt, onion juice or chives, lemon rind and juice.
5 Cut the ham and cucumber into fairly small dice.

6 Add these to the soup with the cream. Serve well chilled.
Variation:
Use finely grated orange rind and juice instead of the lemon.

Fresh tomato juice

You will need for 3-4 servings:
METRIC/IMPERIAL
450 g/1 lb ripe fresh tomatoes
3 spring onions
1 teaspoon oil
1 teaspoon Worcestershire sauce
2 teaspoons castor sugar
seasoning
fresh mint (optional)

1 Wash the tomatoes and chop roughly.
2 Trim spring onions and slice.
3 Place oil in a saucepan with the onions and tomatoes.
4 Cover and cook gently for 10 minutes.
5 Add remaining ingredients, sieve or liquidise.
6 Add 300 ml/½ pint cold water and ice cubes.
7 If liked, decorate each glass with a sprig of fresh mint.

Main Dishes

Mixed vegetable dishes

Vegetable crumble

You will need for 4 servings:

METRIC/IMPERIAL
salt
1 large aubergine
100 g/4 oz streaky
  bacon
1 large onion
50 g/2 oz butter
1 clove garlic, crushed
225 g/8 oz small
  button mushrooms,
  washed
4 tomatoes

freshly ground black
  pepper
50 g/2 oz fresh white
  breadcrumbs
50 g/2 oz grated
  cheese
50 g/2 oz walnuts,
  chopped
1 tablespoon chopped
  parsley

1 Wash the aubergine and cut it into cubes. Sprinkle with salt and leave to stand for 30 minutes, then rinse and drain thoroughly.
2 Remove the rind from the bacon and chop. Peel and slice the onion.
3 Melt the butter in a pan, add the garlic, bacon and onion and cook gently until the onion is soft.
4 Add the aubergine and continue cooking, stirring continuously, until that is also just soft.
5 Stir in the cleaned mushrooms and cook for a few minutes.
6 Skin the tomatoes and cut into quarters.
7 Season the vegetables and stir in the tomatoes. Place in an ovenproof dish.
8 Mix together the breadcrumbs, cheese, walnuts and parsley. Sprinkle over the vegetables and brown under a preheated grill.

Variation:

Use unsalted peanuts instead of walnuts and add $\frac{1}{2}$ teaspoon dried mixed herbs.

Vegetable casserole

You will need for 4-5 servings:

METRIC/IMPERIAL
225 g/8 oz turnip,
  diced
225 g/8 oz onions,
  sliced
100 g/4 oz parsnip, cut
  into strips
1 teaspoon dried
  thyme or mixed
  herbs
350 g/12 oz carrots,
  cut into rings

3 teaspoons Marmite
3 tablespoons
  cornflour
450 g/1 lb potatoes,
  peeled and thinly
  sliced
25 g/1 oz margarine,
  melted

1 Place the diced turnip in the base of a fairly large casserole; cover with the sliced onions and parsnip.
2 Sprinkle with the dried thyme or mixed herbs, cover with the sliced carrots.
3 Dissolve the Marmite in 900 ml/1½ pints boiling water.
4 Blend the cornflour with a little water then pour on some of the hot stock, place the remaining Marmite stock in a saucepan and add the blended cornflour.
5 Bring to the boil to thicken and clear. Pour over the vegetables.
6 Arrange sliced potato on top and brush with the melted margarine.
7 Cover and cook in a moderate oven (150°C, 300°F, Gas Mark 2) for 1 hour, remove lid and cook for a further 30 minutes to brown the potato.

Vegetable moussaka

You will need for 4-5 servings:

METRIC/IMPERIAL
450 g/1 lb new
  potatoes
2 medium-sized
  onions, chopped
4 tablespoons oil
225 g/8 oz cabbage
½ teaspoon salt
pepper
¼ teaspoon diced
  thyme
300 ml/½ pint water
100 g/4 oz
  mushrooms,
  washed

225 g/8 oz tomatoes,
  sliced
for the sauce:
40 g/1½ oz butter or
  margarine
40 g/1½ oz flour
300 ml/½ pint milk
25 g/1 oz grated
  Parmesan cheese

1 Scrub potatoes and cook with their skins on until parboiled, about 10 minutes depending on size. Peel.
2 Cook the onions and oil in a large saucepan until soft but not browned.
3 Wash and shred the cabbage, add to the onion with the salt, pepper and thyme.
4 Add the water, bring to the boil and simmer gently for 10-15 minutes until the cabbage is cooked but still slightly crisp. Remove pan from the heat.
5 Slice the potatoes and add half to the pan, turn half of this mixture into a casserole.
6 Slice the mushrooms and arrange in the casserole.
7 Arrange the sliced tomatoes over the top.
8 Cover with the remaining sliced potatoes.

9 To make the sauce, melt the butter or margarine in a saucepan, add the flour, cook for 1 minute and gradually add the milk. Cook for 2 minutes. Season and pour over the potatoes.
10 Sprinkle over the cheese.
11 Cook in a moderate oven (180°C, 350°F, Gas Mark 4) for about 20 minutes.
12 Serve with a green salad.
Variations:
1 Use different herbs instead of thyme. Try celery seed.
2 Instead of making the sauce, mix the Parmesan with an egg yolk and a (142-ml/5-fl oz) carton of soured cream together and pour over the top before placing in the oven.

Mixed vegetable ring

You will need for 4 servings:
METRIC/IMPERIAL

225 g/8 oz onions	2 large eggs
25 g/1 oz margarine	2 tablespoons top of
1 tablespoon oil	milk
225 g/8 oz frozen	100 g/4 oz grated
mixed vegetables,	Cheddar cheese
thawed	*to garnish:*
50 g/2 oz fresh white	175 g/6 oz carrots,
breadcrumbs	coarsely grated
seasoning	watercress
½ teaspoon dried	
thyme	

1 Prepare and chop onions.
2 Melt the margarine in a saucepan, add the oil and cook the onions slowly for about 5 minutes without browning.
3 Add the vegetables, cover and cook slowly for 10 minutes, shaking the pan occasionally.
4 Stir in breadcrumbs, seasoning and dried thyme, cook for a few minutes and remove from the heat.
5 Beat the eggs with the milk and add with the cheese to the vegetables.
6 Lightly grease a 600-ml/1-pint ring mould.
7 Spoon in the vegetable mixture, level the surface and press down lightly.
8 Cover mould with greaseproof paper and place in a roasting tin half filled with water.
9 Bake in a moderate oven (180°C, 350°F, Gas Mark 4) for 30 minutes until set.
10 Turn out onto a serving dish, fill the centre with grated carrot and decorate dish with sprigs of watercress.

Vegetable pudding

You will need for 3-4 servings:
METRIC/IMPERIAL

1 kg/2 lb swedes or	½ teaspoon nutmeg
turnips	1½ teaspoons salt
100 g/4 oz fresh white	pepper
breadcrumbs	2 eggs, lightly beaten
50 ml/2 fl oz single	25 g/1 oz butter
cream	

1 Peel and chop the vegetables. Cook in boiling salted water until soft, about 20 minutes.
2 Drain and mash.
3 Add the breadcrumbs, cream, nutmeg, seasonings and beaten eggs. Mix well.
4 Pour into a well-buttered ovenproof dish, dot with the butter.
5 Cook in a moderate oven (180°C, 350°F, Gas Mark 4) for 1 hour until firm to the touch.

Leek and lentil supper dish

You will need for 4-5 servings:
METRIC/IMPERIAL

350 g/12 oz dried	seasoning
lentils	450 g/1 lb leeks
1 kg/2 lb potatoes	2 large eggs
50 g/2 oz butter or	100 g/4 oz Edam
margarine	cheese, grated

1 Cook the lentils in 900 ml/1½ pints of water, bring to the boil stirring and cook fairly quickly for 20 minutes, stirring occasionally. Drain well.
2 Peel potatoes, slice and cook in salted water until tender. Drain well and mash with 25 g/1 oz of the butter or margarine. Season well.
3 Trim the leeks and wash very thoroughly to remove grit. Slice thinly.
4 Melt the remaining butter or margarine in a saucepan, add the leeks, cover and cook very gently for 5-10 minutes, then stir in the lentils.
5 Beat the eggs and add 75 g/3 oz of the cheese; stir into the leek and lentil mixture.
6 Arrange the mashed potato at each end of an ovenproof dish.
7 Place the leek and lentil mixture in the centre.
8 Sprinkle with the remaining cheese.
9 Cook in a moderate oven (180°C, 350°F, Gas Mark 4) for 15 minutes to heat through.
10 Serve with a tomato salad.

Lentil and nut loaf

You will need for 4 servings:
METRIC/IMPERIAL

100 g/4 oz lentils	seasoning
3 teaspoons Marmite	*for the sauce:*
50 g/2 oz margarine	50 g/2 oz margarine
175 g/6 oz onions,	175 g/6 oz onions,
chopped	finely chopped
½ teaspoon dried	4 fresh bay leaves
mixed herbs	50 g/2 oz flour
2 tablespoons flour	450 ml/¾ pint milk
175 g/6 oz milled nuts	seasoning
(any mixed nuts)	*to garnish:*
2 eggs, well beaten	watercress

1 Wash lentils thoroughly and drain, place in a small saucepan and cover with water, about 300 ml/½ pint.
2 Bring to the boil and stir in the Marmite; simmer for 7-10 minutes until soft, strain and keep on one side.

3 Melt the margarine, add onions and herbs, cover and cook gently for 10 minutes.

4 Stir in the flour and remaining ingredients and mix well.

5 Lightly grease and line a 450 g/1 lb loaf tin, place the mixture in the tin and level the surface.

6 Bake on the upper shelf of a preheated moderate oven (180°C, 350°F, Gas Mark 4) for 40 minutes.

7 Meanwhile, make the sauce. Melt the margarine, add the onions and bay leaves, cover and cook until soft without browning, about 10 minutes.

8 Remove the bay leaves, stir in the flour and cook for 2-3 minutes.

9 Gradually stir in the milk, bring to the boil, simmer for 3 minutes and season.

10 Turn the loaf out of the tin and pour the sauce over. Garnish with watercress. Serve with Brussels sprouts, baked tomatoes and either French bread or chips or roast potatoes.

Cheese and potato hot pot

You will need for 4-5 servings:
METRIC/IMPERIAL

50 g/2 oz butter or margarine	100 g/4 oz Cheddar cheese, grated
50 g/2 oz plain flour	¾ kg/1½ lb potatoes, thinly sliced
2 teaspoons Marmite	
600 ml/1 pint milk	
pepper	
175 g/6 oz onions, finely chopped	

1 Make a sauce by melting the butter or margarine; add the flour and Marmite. Stir to dissolve.

2 Gradually add the milk, beating to a smooth consistency each time, bring to the boil, add the pepper and onions and cook for a few minutes.

3 Stir in 75 g/3 oz of the cheese.

4 Using a well-buttered 1.25-litre/2-pint ovenproof dish, layer the potatoes and sauce alternately, ending with a layer of sauce; sprinkle with remaining cheese.

5 Bake covered with foil in a moderately hot oven (190°C, 375°F, Gas Mark 5) for 1½ hours.

Potato and bean pie

You will need for 4 servings:
METRIC/IMPERIAL

750 g/1½ lb potatoes	100 g/4 oz Cheddar cheese
50 g/2 oz margarine	pepper
50 g/2 oz flour	1 (350-g/12-oz) packet frozen sliced green beans, thawed
600 ml/1 pint milk	
2 teaspoons Marmite	
175 g/6 oz onions, chopped	

1 Peel and slice potatoes fairly thinly.

2 To make the sauce, melt the margarine, add the flour and cook for 2 minutes. Gradually beat in the milk, bring to the boil and cook for about 3 minutes.

3 Stir in the Marmite, making sure it dissolves; add the onions, three-quarters of the cheese and pepper.

4 Fill a fairly deep ovenproof dish with alternate layers of potatoes, green beans and sauce, ending with a layer of sauce. Sprinkle with remaining cheese.

5 Cover with foil and cook in a moderately hot oven (190°C, 375°F, Gas Mark 5) for about 1 hour.

Potato and carrot layer pie

You will need for 4 servings:
METRIC/IMPERIAL

4 large eggs	350 g/12 oz carrots
1 kg/2 lb potatoes	¼ teaspoon dried sage seasoning
350 g/12 oz onions	
75 g/3 oz butter or margarine	25 g/1 oz plain flour
	150 ml/¼ pint milk

1 Cook the eggs in boiling water for 10 minutes. Drain, crack and cover with cold water.

2 Peel the potatoes, cut into even sizes, cover with cold salted water, bring to the boil and cook for 10 minutes.

3 Prepare and slice onions.

4 Melt 50 g/2 oz of the butter or margarine, add the onions and cook without browning for 10 minutes.

5 Meanwhile, peel and finely slice the carrots. Add them to the onion with 3 tablespoons water and cook gently for 10 minutes.

6 Stir in the sage and seasoning.

7 Add the flour and cook for 2 minutes; then gradually stir in the milk and cook until thickened, about 3 minutes.

8 Slice the potatoes and arrange half in the base of a flameproof dish.

9 Slice the eggs and arrange over the potato.

10 Cover this with the onion and carrot mixture.

11 Arrange the remaining sliced potatoes neatly over the surface.

12 Melt the remaining butter or margarine and use to brush over the potatoes.

13 Place the dish under a moderate grill to heat through and lightly brown the potatoes.

Variation:
Sprinkle a little grated cheese over the top.

Vegetable cottage pie

You will need for 4 servings:
METRIC/IMPERIAL

50 g/2 oz margarine	225 g/8 oz carrots
2 tablespoons oil	50 g/2 oz peanuts
225 g/8 oz onions, chopped	3 tablespoons dry parsley and thyme stuffing mix
350 g/12 oz mushrooms, chopped	1 tablespoon tomato ketchup
1 tablespoon Marmite	seasoning
450 g/1 lb potatoes	

1 Place 40 g/1½ oz of the margarine in a saucepan with the oil and onions; cook gently for 10 minutes until soft.
2 Stir in the mushrooms, cook for 5 minutes and stir in the Marmite.
3 Meanwhile, peel and slice potatoes and carrots and cook in boiling salted water until just soft.
4 Remove the carrots and mince with the peanuts; stir them into the mushrooms with the dry stuffing mix, ketchup and seasoning.
5 Place in a 1.25-litre/2-pint pie dish.
6 Drain the potatoes and mash with the remaining margarine and seasoning.
7 Spread over the vegetable mixture.
8 Cook in a moderately hot oven (190°C, 375°F, Gas Mark 5) for 40 minutes.

Winter vegetable pie

You will need for 4-6 servings:

METRIC/IMPERIAL

450 g/1 lb potatoes	*for the sauce:*
450 g/1 lb parsnips	50 g/2 oz butter or
450 g/1 lb carrots	margarine
50 g/2 oz butter or	50 g/2 oz plain flour
margarine	450 ml/¾ pint milk
2 tablespoons oil	100 g/4 oz strong
½ teaspoon dried	Cheddar cheese,
thyme	grated
seasoning	melted butter

1 Peel the potatoes and cook in boiling salted water for 10 minutes. They need to be firm enough to slice.
2 Peel and coarsely grate the carrots and parsnips.
3 Melt butter or margarine and oil in a saucepan, add the grated vegetables, stir round and cover with a disc of greaseproof paper and the saucepan lid. Cook gently for 15 minutes, stirring occasionally.
4 Add the thyme and seasoning and arrange in an ovenproof dish.
5 For the sauce, melt the butter or margarine, add the flour and cook for 1 minute.
6 Gradually add the milk, beating well each time to give a smooth consistency.
7 Bring to the boil, stirring, simmer and cook for 2 minutes.
8 Stir in the cheese and pour over the vegetables.
9 Slice the potatoes fairly thinly and arrange slightly overlapping over the pie.
10 Brush potatoes with melted butter and place under a moderate grill to heat through, about 10-15 minutes.

Vegetable fiesta

You will need for 6 servings:

METRIC/IMPERIAL

1 medium-sized	1 (597-g/14-oz) can
onion, sliced	artichoke hearts,
350 g/12 oz	drained and quartered
courgettes, sliced	25 g/1 oz butter
into 1-cm/½-inch	25 g/1 oz flour
slices	1 egg, beaten
1 small aubergine,	3 tablespoons top of
sliced into cubes	the milk
450 ml/¾ pint water	*to garnish:*
2 chicken stock cubes	8 stuffed green olives,
1 teaspoon salt	sliced

1 Put onion, courgettes and aubergine in a pan with the water and stock cubes.
2 Add the salt and bring to the boil, cover, reduce heat and simmer until just tender, about 10-15 minutes.
3 Drain, reserving the liquid.
4 Arrange the vegetables in an ovenproof serving dish and add the artichoke hearts and keep hot.
5 Blend the butter and flour together to a smooth paste.
6 Stir into the hot reserved liquid and bring to the boil, stirring until thickened.
7 Cool slightly, add the egg and top of the milk and stir to blend.
8 Reheat to just under boiling point, check for seasoning and pour over the vegetables.
9 Garnish with the sliced olives and serve.

Bacon pan-fry

You will need for 3-4 servings:

METRIC/IMPERIAL

225 g/8 oz middlecut	freshly ground pepper
or streaky bacon	25 g/1 oz butter
rashers	1 tablespoon oil
1 large onion,	*to garnish:*
chopped	fried onion rings
750 g/1½ lb potatoes	(optional)
1 large egg	

1 Remove the rind from the bacon and cut the rashers into pieces.
2 Put in a frying pan with the onion and fry gently to extract the fat from the bacon, adding a little butter if required.
3 Cook for 15 minutes to soften the onion without browning. Remove and keep on one side.
4 Peel the potatoes, halve and parboil them in boiling salted water for about 5-10 minutes. (The success of this dish depends on the potatoes not becoming floury and soft). Drain and cool slightly.
5 Coarsely grate potatoes into a bowl, add the bacon and onion, the well-beaten egg, and plenty of pepper. Stir gently.
6 Melt the butter and oil in a small omelette pan, press the potato mixture into the pan and cook gently until

the underside is nicely browned, about 10-12 minutes.

7 Place under a moderate grill for 5-10 minutes to slightly brown the top and to finish cooking the centre.

8 If liked, garnish with fried onion rings.

Vegetable hotpot with frankfurters

You will need for 4 servings:

METRIC/IMPERIAL

1 small green pepper	150 ml/¼ pint dry red wine
1 large onion	
3 sticks celery	2 potatoes, peeled and cubed
2 carrots	
3 tablespoons oil	100 g/4 oz button mushrooms
1 large clove garlic, crushed	
salt	1 (312-g/11-oz) can sweetcorn
freshly ground black pepper	225 g/8 oz frankfurters, cut into chunks
1 tablespoon flour	
½ chicken stock cube	100 g/4 oz frozen peas
150 ml/¼ pint water	2 tablespoons parsley

1 Remove the seeds, pith and stalk from the green pepper and slice.

2 Peel the onion and slice.

3 Trim the celery and carrots and slice both.

4 Heat the oil in a deep frying pan or skillet, add the garlic and prepared vegetables and cook until the onion is soft. Season with salt and freshly ground black pepper.

5 Stir in the flour and cook, stirring continuously, for a few minutes.

6 Dissolve the chicken stock cube in the water then stir into the vegetables together with the red wine.

7 Add the potatoes, cover and simmer gently for 20-30 minutes, until the vegetables are cooked.

8 10 minutes before the end of the cooking time, add the remaining ingredients.

9 Serve with French bread.

Vegetable curry

You will need for 4-5 servings:

METRIC/IMPERIAL

3 tablespoons corn oil	pinch sugar
225 g/8 oz onions, chopped	1 small cauliflower
1½ tablespoons curry powder	225 g/8 oz Brussels sprouts
50 g/2 oz plain flour	4 sticks celery
1 tablespoon Marmite	3 tomatoes
900 ml/1½ pints hot water	seasoning
	to serve:
1 small clove garlic, crushed (optional)	plain boiled rice
	salted peanuts
1 tablespoon tomato purée	banana
	coconut
	mango chutney

1 Place the oil and onions in a large pan and cook until soft without browning, about 10 minutes.

2 Stir in the curry powder and cook very gently for 5 minutes.

3 Stir in the flour and cook for 1 minute.

4 Gradually add the Marmite dissolved in the hot water, bring to the boil, stirring, and cook for 2 minutes.

5 Add the garlic if used, tomato purée and sugar. Remove pan from the heat.

6 Wash the cauliflower and divide into sprigs; prepare the sprouts and celery and cut into 2-cm/1-inch pieces.

7 Add the vegetables to the pan and cook slowly, stirring occasionally, for about 10-15 minutes, until just tender.

8 Cut the tomatoes into segments and add with seasoning to taste.

9 Cook for a further 5 minutes.

10 Serve with plain boiled rice accompanied by salted peanuts, banana, coconut and mango chutney.

Vegetable fondue

You will need for 4 servings:

METRIC/IMPERIAL

50 g/2 oz butter	1 (320-g/11½-oz) can sweetcorn
100 g/4 oz streaky bacon, chopped	
	salt
3 carrots, peeled and chopped	freshly ground black pepper
1 large onion, peeled and chopped	for dipping:
	small cooked sausages
2 sticks celery, sliced	
1 clove garlic, crushed	small meatballs
225 g/8 oz cauliflower florets, washed	pieces of French bread
300 ml/½ pint dry cider	roughly chopped hard-boiled egg
150 ml/¼ pint water	
½ chicken stock cube	cubes of Cheddar cheese
100 g/4 oz button mushrooms, sliced	stuffed olives

1 Melt the butter in a saucepan, add the prepared bacon, carrots, onion, celery and garlic. Cook gently until the bacon is cooked and the onion soft, about 10 minutes.

2 Add the cauliflower, cider, water and stock cube. Bring to the boil and simmer for 20 minutes.

3 Cool slightly, then liquidise until smooth. Add the mushrooms and sweetcorn (including the liquid from the can).

4 Taste and season with salt and pepper if necessary.

5 Prepare a selection of foods to dip, reheat the fondue in a heavy based or earthenware fondue pan and keep hot over a low burner.

Variation:

50g/2 oz grated cheese may be stirred into the fondue, together with 2 teaspoons caraway seeds.

One-vegetable recipes

Chicory and ham mornay

You will need for 3-4 servings:

METRIC/IMPERIAL

3 medium heads chicory	seasoning
70 g/2½ oz butter or margarine	6 slices ham
	40 g/1½ oz flour
	450 ml/¾ pint milk

1 Wash the chicory and remove any damaged outside leaves; cut in half lengthwise.
2 Using 40 g/1½ oz of the butter spread each half with a little butter and season.
3 Wrap each piece of chicory in a slice of ham and place in an ovenproof dish.
4 Make the sauce by melting the remaining butter or margarine in a saucepan.
5 Stir in the flour and cook for 1 minute.
6 Gradually blend in the milk, making sure there are no lumps.
7 Bring to the boil, stirring, and cook for 2 minutes.
8 Pour over the chicory and place in a preheated moderately hot oven (190°C, 375°F, Gas Mark 5) on the centre shelf for 35-40 minutes until tender.

Variations:

1 Instead of a plain white sauce, make a cheese sauce.
2 Add dried thyme to the white sauce.
3 Sprinkle lightly with a little grated cheese.
4 Garnish with slices of tomato for extra colour.

Leeks au gratin

You will need for 3 servings:

METRIC/IMPERIAL

6 medium leeks	1 tablespoon tomato purée
for the sauce:	
1 tablespoon corn oil	½ teaspoon dried thyme
100 g/4 oz onions, chopped	6 slices shoulder of ham
225 g/8 oz tomatoes	25 g/1 oz Cheddar cheese, grated
1 teaspoon Marmite	
seasoning	
pinch sugar	

1 Trim and wash the leeks very thoroughly to remove any grit.
2 Cook in boiling salted water until just tender, 10-15 minutes depending on size.
3 Drain well, then place on kitchen paper and keep hot.
4 Place oil and onions in a small saucepan and cook for 5 minutes.
5 Add the roughly chopped tomatoes and cook until mushy, about 10 minutes.
6 Stir in the Marmite, seasoning, sugar, tomato purée and thyme.
7 Wrap each leek in a slice of ham and place in an ovenproof dish.
8 Spoon the sauce over the leeks and sprinkle with the cheese.
9 Place the dish under a moderate grill to reheat the leeks and just melt the cheese.

Savoury cauliflower cheese

You will need for 3-4 servings:

METRIC/IMPERIAL

1 medium cauliflower	2 teaspoons Marmite
40 g/1½ oz butter or margarine	75 g/3 oz Cheddar cheese, grated
25 g/1 oz plain flour	
300 ml/½ pint milk	

1 Trim the cauliflower and cut into sprigs, or leave whole.
2 Cook in boiling salted water until just tender. Drain well and place in a heated ovenproof dish.
3 Meanwhile, make a sauce in the usual way with the butter or margarine, flour and milk.
4 Stir in the Marmite and some of the cheese. Pour the sauce over the cauliflower and if liked sprinkle with the remaining grated cheese.
5 Lightly brown under the grill.

Cauliflower savoury

You will need for 4 servings:

METRIC/IMPERIAL

1 kg/2 lb cauliflower	25 g/1 oz plain flour
1 medium onion	150 ml/¼ pint milk
25 g/1 oz butter or margarine	*for the topping:*
100 g/4 oz streaky bacon	25 g/1 oz grated Parmesan cheese
100 g/4 oz mushrooms	1 tablespoon browned breadcrumbs
seasoning	
for the sauce:	
40 g/1½ oz butter or margarine	

1 Wash and trim the cauliflower, remove the thick stalk and divide into sprigs.
2 Bring a large pan of salted water to the boil and cook the cauliflower until just crisp.
3 Drain the cauliflower, reserving 150 ml/¼ pint of the liquor.
4 Prepare and chop the onion.
5 Melt the butter or margarine, add the onion and cook slowly until soft without browning.
6 Remove rind from the bacon and cut into pieces, add to the onion.

7 Wash and chop the mushrooms.
8 Add to the onion and cook for 3 minutes.
9 Stir in seasoning and spread mixture over the base of an ovenproof dish.
10 Arrange the drained cauliflower over the top.
11 To make the sauce, melt the butter or margarine in a saucepan, add the flour and cook gently for 2 minutes.
12 Mix the milk and reserved cauliflower water together and gradually add to the flour, blending in well with each addition.
13 Bring to the boil, stirring, and cook for 3 minutes.
14 Season the sauce and pour over the cauliflower.
15 Sprinkle with the cheese and crumbs; place the dish under a preheated grill to brown lightly.

Variations:
1 Add a little grated blue cheese to the sauce.
2 Add dried thyme to the bacon and onion mixture.
3 Add a little yeast extract to the bacon and onion mixture.

Cauliflower fritters with special sauce

You will need for 4 servings:
METRIC/IMPERIAL

1 large cauliflower	pepper and salt
salt	100 g/4 oz cream
for the sauce:	cheese
1 medium onion, thinly sliced	oil for deep frying
50 g/2 oz butter or margarine	*for the batter:*
225 g/8 oz tomatoes, peeled	100 g/4 oz plain flour
½ teaspoon dried mixed herbs or basil	1 tablespoon oil
	150 ml/¼ pint tepid water
	2 egg whites

1 Prepare cauliflower, discarding all the green, and break into sprigs.
2 Place in a large pan of salted water, bring to the boil and cook until just tender, 5-10 minutes depending on the size.
3 Drain and refresh in cold water to cool. Dry on kitchen paper.
4 To make the sauce, fry the onion in the butter or margarine until soft for about 10 minutes without browning.
5 Chop the tomatoes, add to the onion with the herbs, pepper, salt and cook gently for 10 minutes.
6 Remove pan from the heat and gradually beat in the cream cheese until it is blended. Keep on one side.
7 Prepare deep fat pan, heat the oil to 180°C, 350°F, or until a piece of bread chopped and dropped in cooks to a golden colour in 10 seconds.
8 Meanwhile, make the fritter batter. Blend the flour, oil, water and a pinch of salt together until a smooth consistency. Beat well.
9 Whisk the egg whites until stiff and fold into the batter mixture.

10 Dip the cauliflower in the batter, turning in the batter with 2 skewers to coat completely.
11 Lift out one at a time and fry a few at a time for 3-4 minutes.
12 Remove with a slotted spoon and drain on kitchen paper. Keep hot until all the florets are fried.
13 Reheat the sauce and serve at once.

Blue cheese cauliflower

You will need for 4 servings:
METRIC/IMPERIAL

1 medium-sized cauliflower	40 g/1½ oz flour
50 g/2 oz streaky bacon	300 ml/½ pint milk
	seasoning
100 g/4 oz Danish Blue cheese	15 g/½ oz potato crisps, crushed
40 g/1½ oz butter, unsalted	

1 Break the cauliflower into sprigs and cook in a little boiling salted water until just tender. Drain and reserve 150 ml/¼ pint of the stock. Place cauliflower in a serving dish.
2 Remove rind from the bacon, cut into strips and fry until crisp. Remove and drain on kitchen paper.
3 Crumble the cheese into a pan, add butter, flour, milk and reserved liquor.
4 Stir over medium heat until thick and season to taste.
5 Pour the sauce over the cauliflower; sprinkle with the crushed crisps and cooked bacon.
6 Cook in a moderately hot oven (200°C, 400°F, Gas Mark 6) for 15 minutes.
7 Serve with a green salad.

Cauliflower surprise

You will need for 4 servings:
METRIC/IMPERIAL

1 large cauliflower	25 g/1 oz grated Parmesan cheese
25 g/1 oz butter or margarine	25 g/1 oz Brazil nuts or hazelnuts
1 tablespoon oil	
for the sauce:	*for the topping:*
65 g/2½ oz butter or margarine	75 g/3 oz fresh breadcrumbs
65 g/2½ oz plain flour	15 g/½ oz butter
600 ml/1 pint milk	
seasoning	
100 g/4 oz Emmenthal cheese, grated	

1 Wash cauliflower, remove coarse outer leaves and cut away thick stalk.
2 Divide cauliflower into florets; finely chop remaining leaves and any small leaves.
3 Melt butter or margarine and oil in a saucepan.

4 Add cauliflower, stir well, cover and cook gently for 10-15 minutes, stirring occasionally.
5 Drain cauliflower, reserving the liquor, and arrange cauliflower in an ovenproof dish.
6 To make the sauce, melt butter or margarine in small pan, stir in flour and cook for 2 minutes.
7 Remove from the heat and gradually beat in the milk. Bring to the boil, stirring and cook for 2 minutes until thickened.
8 Add the cauliflower liquor, seasoning to taste. Remove from the heat.
9 Add half the grated Emmenthal and Parmesan.
10 Slice the nuts and add.
11 Pour over the cauliflower.
12 Mix the remaining cheese and breadcrumbs together and sprinkle over the cauliflower. Dot with the remaining butter.
13 Place dish in grill pan and grill gently for 15 minutes to heat through.
14 Serve with a green salad.

Baked mushrooms

You will need for 4 servings:

METRIC/IMPERIAL

450 g/1 lb button mushrooms, washed	½ teaspoon salt pepper
1 small onion, chopped	1 (142-ml/5-fl oz) carton soured cream
50 g/2 oz butter or margarine	¼ teaspoon Worcestershire sauce
2 teaspoons plain flour	

1 Dry the mushrooms and slice.
2 Cook the onion and butter or margarine in a pan for 2 minutes, add the mushrooms, cover and cook gently for 5 minutes.
3 Sprinkle in the flour and seasoning and cook for 2 minutes.
4 Remove pan from the heat and stir in the remaining ingredients.
5 Lightly butter an ovenproof dish and put in the mushroom mixture.
6 Bake in a moderate oven (180°C, 350°F, Gas Mark 4) for 15 minutes.
7 Serve with noodles and green salad.

Potato gratin

You will need for 4 servings:

METRIC/IMPERIAL

750 g-1 kg/1½-2 lb potatoes	seasoning
1 medium onion	300 ml/½ pint milk
	25 g/1 oz butter

1 Peel the potatoes and slice very thinly.
2 Prepare and slice the onion.

3 Thickly butter a 1-litre/2-pint casserole dish.
4 Arrange alternate layers of potato and onion in the dish, carefully seasoning every alternate layer.
5 Finish with a layer of potatoes.
6 Pour over the milk and dot with the butter.
7 Place in a preheated moderate oven (180°C, 350°F, Gas Mark 4) on the centre shelf for 2 hours.
8 Halfway through the cooking time, tip the dish and spoon some of the milk over the top to help the browning.

Variations:

1 Sprinkle with a few fresh or dried herbs.
2 Add chopped chives with the onion.
3 Fry bacon crisply, crumble and add with the onion.
4 Sprinkle some grated cheese over the top or in the layers.
5 Use 2 leeks finely sliced instead of the onions.
6 Add an egg yolk to the milk.
7 To serve as a meal on its own, cover layers with a cheese sauce.
8 For a supper dish, put some bacon rashers in the layers.

Individual sweetcorn bakes

You will need for 6 servings:

METRIC/IMPERIAL

6 slices buttered brown bread, crusts removed	seasoning
100 g/4 oz cream cheese	6 rashers streaky bacon
1 (320-g/11½-oz) can sweetcorn	to garnish: lettuce leaves sprigs of watercress
1 tablespoon chopped chives	

1 Place each slice of bread, buttered side down, in 10cm/4-inch individual Yorkshire pudding tins. Preheat the oven to moderately hot (200°C, 400°F, Gas Mark 6).
2 Mix the cream cheese with the strained sweetcorn, chives and seasoning.
3 Fill the bread-lined tins with this mixture. Remove the rind from the bacon and roll each rasher up. Secure with a wooden cocktail stick before placing on top of the sweetcorn mixture.
4 Bake for 15-20 minutes until crisp and golden.
5 Serve on crisp lettuce leaves and garnish with watercress.

Stuffed vegetables

Spanish baked aubergines

You will need for 4 servings:

METRIC/IMPERIAL

4 medium-sized
  aubergines
for the filling:
25 g/1 oz butter
1 large onion,
  chopped
2 cloves garlic,
  crushed
1 (397-g/14-oz) can
  tomatoes
1 teaspoon brown
  sugar

seasoning
25 g/1 oz stuffed
  green olives, sliced
for the topping:
25 g/1 oz grated
  cheese
25 g/1 oz chopped
  nuts
25 g/1 oz white
  breadcrumbs

1 Cut each aubergine in half, scoop out centre line of seeds using a teaspoon, leaving a trough in each for the filling.

2 Arrange in a greased fairly shallow dish so that the halves fit in neatly.

3 Melt butter for the filling and cook the onion and garlic slowly without colouring until transparent and tender; add the canned tomatoes, scooped out aubergine pulp and sugar and season well. Turn up the heat and cook briskly, stirring until the mixture has reduced to a thickish pulp; add the olives. Spoon filling into the aubergine halves; it may spill over a bit if the halves are small ones. Mix together the cheese, nuts and breadcrumbs and sprinkle the mixture over the top.

4 Bake in a moderately hot oven (190°C, 375°F, Gas Mark 5) for about 40 minutes until the top is brown and the aubergines are tender.

Stuffed cabbage leaves

You will need for 4 servings:

METRIC/IMPERIAL

75 g/3 oz long-grain
  rice
1 medium-sized onion
2 tablespoons corn oil
225 g/8 oz cooked
  lamb
seasoning
1 teaspoon oregano
2 teaspoons chopped
  fresh mint
8 large cabbage
  leaves

for the sauce:
300 ml/½ pint cabbage
  water plus 1
  vegetable stock
  cube
juice of ½ lemon
25 g/1 oz butter or
  margarine
25 g/1 oz plain flour

1 Cook the rice in plenty of boiling salted water for 12-15 minutes until just tender. Drain well.

2 Chop the onion and place in a frying pan with the oil.

3 Fry gently until just beginning to brown, about 10 minutes.

4 Trim the lamb and cut into small dice.

5 Add the lamb and rice to the frying pan and mix in the seasoning and herbs. Keep on one side.

6 Trim the hard stalks from the cabbage leaves, cover the leaves with boiling water and leave for 5 minutes.

7 Remove and drain well, reserving the stock, and spread each leaf flat.

8 Divide the lamb and rice filling among the leaves, press the filling together and roll up the leaves tightly to completely enclose the filling.

9 Place close together in the frying pan.

10 Make up the stock and pour into the pan with the lemon juice.

11 Cover and simmer very gently for 20 minutes.

12 Remove cabbage leaves and put in a heated serving dish.

13 Melt the butter or margarine in a small saucepan, stir in the flour and cook for 1 minute.

14 Strain off the stock from the frying pan and gradually add to the flour, bring to the boil, stirring, and simmer for 3 minutes.

15 Serve with the stuffed cabbage leaves and some carrots.

Variations:

1 Add a few chopped brazil nuts and sultanas to the rice.

2 The cabbage parcels may be cooked in tomato juice and a little cabbage water. Make the sauce in the same way, adding a little sugar.

3 Fresh chopped or crushed rosemary may be added to the rice instead of the oregano and mint.

Stuffed fennel

You will need for 4 servings:

METRIC/IMPERIAL

4 heads fennel,
  washed and
  trimmed
1 onion
100 g/4 oz cooked
  chicken
225 g/8 oz chicken
  livers
100 g/4 oz butter
5 tablespoons port
seasoning
2 tablespoons flour
300 ml/½ pint chicken
  stock

to garnish:
bunches of fennel
  leaves

1 Cook the fennel in boiling salted water for 20 minutes until soft.

2 Peel and finely chop the onion; chop the cooked chicken and the chicken livers.

3 Melt half the butter in a pan, add the onion and livers

and cook thoroughly, stirring continuously. Add the cooked chicken and 2 tablespoons of the port. Season.

4 Drain the fennel and carefully cut out some of the heart to form a hollow. Chop this removed fennel and add to the chicken mixture. Refill the fennel with this mixture. Keep warm.

5 Melt the remaining butter in a pan, add the flour and cook for a few minutes; then stir in the stock and remaining port. Bring to the boil and cook for 2 minutes and serve in a warm sauce boat.

6 Garnish the stuffed fennel with the reserved fennel leaves before serving.

Stuffed marrow

You will need for 4 servings:

METRIC/IMPERIAL

1 medium-sized marrow	1 teaspoon dried mixed herbs
1 onion	seasoning
1 clove garlic (optional)	2 tablespoons Parmesan cheese
1 tablespoon corn oil	
450 g/1 lb minced beef	
100 g/4 oz aubergine	
50 g/2 oz mushrooms	
3 medium-sized tomatoes	
2 teaspoons tomato purée	

1 Trim the ends from the marrow, peel the marrow and cut in half lengthways.
2 Scoop out the soft pith in the centre with a spoon.
3 Bring a large pan of salted water to the boil and cook the marrow for 5 minutes until just tender but still crisp. Remove and drain well.
4 Place in an ovenproof dish to cool.
5 Peel and chop the onion and crush the garlic.
6 Place the oil in a frying pan, add the onion and garlic if used and cook for 10 minutes to soften without browning, stirring occasionally. Add the mince.
7 Cut the ends off the aubergine and chop the flesh coarsely.
8 Wash and chop mushrooms and add to the pan with the aubergine.
9 Skin and chop the tomatoes, add to the mince with the purée, herbs and seasoning.
10 Stir and cook for 15 minutes.
11 Divide the mixture between the two marrow halves and sprinkle with Parmesan cheese.
12 Cook in a moderate oven (190°C, 375°F, Gas Mark 5) for 40 minutes.
13 Serve with sauté potatoes and a tossed green salad.

Variation:
Omit the aubergine and add 100 g/4 oz cooked rice to the mince before filling the marrow.

Tuna stuffed tomatoes

You will need for 6 servings:

METRIC/IMPERIAL

6 medium tomatoes	2 tablespoons soured cream or mayonnaise (see page 87)
1 (198-g/7-oz) can tuna fish	
100 g/4 oz cream cheese	2 teaspoons chopped chives
1 teaspoon lemon juice	12 (5-cm/2-inch) rounds bread
seasoning	oil for frying

1 Halve the tomatoes and, using a teaspoon, scoop out the centres into a strainer.
2 Turn tomatoes upside down to drain, cutting a piece off the bottom first to make sure they stand level.
3 Drain the liquor from the fish and flake the flesh into a bowl.
4 Stir in the cream cheese, lemon juice, seasoning and the drained tomato pieces, chopping up any large ones.
5 Blend the mixture well and stir in the soured cream or mayonnaise with the chives.
6 Spoon into the tomato halves.
7 Fry the bread rounds in the oil and serve a tomato on each.

Stuffed peppers with ham and eggs

You will need for 4 servings:

METRIC/IMPERIAL

4 even-sized green peppers	3 slices ham, cut into strips
salt	to garnish:
6 large eggs	parsley
seasoning	
little cream or milk	
butter	

1 Cut lids off the tops of the peppers and scoop out the seeds and pith.
2 Place them in a large pan of boiling salted water for 15 minutes.
3 Drain well upside down and place in a buttered ovenproof dish. Keep hot.
4 Beat the eggs, seasoning and milk or cream together.
5 Melt a little butter in a pan and very lightly scramble the eggs so they are still runny but just beginning to set.
6 Add the ham strips, heat gently, and spoon into the pepper shells.
7 Serve garnished with parsley.

Variations:
1 Fry a little onion and bacon and then add the eggs.
2 Serve with a round of tomato on top, sprinkle with cheese and place under grill until the cheese is just melted.

Stuffed green peppers

You will need for 4 servings:

METRIC/IMPERIAL
4 large green peppers
450 g/1 lb raw lean
   minced lamb or veal
1 large Spanish onion
1 tablespoon flour
150 ml/¼ pint water (or
   water and stock
   cube)
¼ teaspoon salt
black pepper
10 stuffed olives,
   coarsely chopped

for the cheese sauce:
25 g/1 oz butter
25 g/1 oz flour
300 ml/½ pint milk
75 g/3 oz grated
   Cheddar cheese
¼ teaspoon salt
pepper
teaspoon made
   mustard
to garnish:
8 extra stuffed green
   olives

1 Cut the core out from the top of the peppers and remove seeds.
2 Fry the minced meat for 1 minute, then add the chopped onion.
3 Cook gently until the onions are soft, then stir in the flour, then the water.
4 Season and bring to the boil for 1 minute.
5 Add the olives.
6 Stuff peppers with the meat mixture and set upright in a casserole just large enough to hold the peppers.
7 Make the cheese sauce by melting the butter in a saucepan.
8 Add the flour and then gradually add the milk.
9 Return to the heat and bring to the boil, stirring.
10 Add the cheese and seasoning and pour round the peppers.
11 Cook in a preheated moderate oven (180°C, 350°F, Gas Mark 4) for 1 hour.
12 Garnish with stuffed olives before serving.

Variation:
Use beef with a few herbs and a little tomato purée added.

Egg dishes and pancakes

Cheese and eggs with onions

You will need for 6 servings:

METRIC/IMPERIAL
350 g/12 oz onions,
   sliced
50 g/2 oz butter or
   margarine
4 hard-boiled eggs
350 g/12 oz potatoes,
   peeled and boiled

25 g/1 oz flour
300 ml/½ pint milk
seasoning
grated nutmeg
75 g/3 oz grated
   cheese

1 Cook the onions in boiling water for 5 minutes, then drain.
2 Melt 25 g/1 oz butter or margarine in a saucepan, add the onions, cover and cook very slowly until tender, about 15 minutes.
3 Sieve or liquidise the onions to give a purée.
4 Slice the eggs and potatoes, mix together and arrange in a flameproof dish.
5 Melt the remaining butter or margarine, add the flour and cook for 1 minute. Gradually stir in the onion purée, milk, salt, pepper and nutmeg, then bring to the boil and pour over the eggs and potatoes.
6 Sprinkle with the cheese and place under a very moderate grill to heat through and brown the cheese, about 10-15 minutes.

Variation:
Mushrooms could also be added.

Marmite tortilla

You will need for 3-4 servings:

METRIC/IMPERIAL
25 g/1 oz butter or
   margarine
1 teaspoon Marmite
175 g/6 oz onions,
   sliced
3 large eggs
3 tablespoons water
pepper
225 g/8 oz cooked
   cold potatoes

125 g/4 oz cooked
   sliced green beans
to garnish:
2 tomatoes, sliced

1 Melt the butter or margarine in a 20-cm/8-inch omelette pan.
2 Stir in the Marmite to dissolve.
3 Add the sliced onions and cook until soft without browning, about 10 minutes.
4 Beat the eggs, water and a little pepper together, pour onto the onion and stir. Add the diced potato and the beans.
5 Cook very slowly so the egg becomes firm and set.
6 Preheat a moderate grill and cook the topside of the omelette, leaving it in the pan and being careful of the handle.
7 Turn out and eat either hot or cold, garnished with sliced tomatoes.

Spanish tortilla omelette

You will need for 4 servings:
METRIC/IMPERIAL
150 ml/¼ pint olive oil
450 g/1 lb large old
  potatoes, peeled,
  cut into thin slices
1½ teaspoons salt
1 large onion, finely
  chopped

75 g/3 oz stuffed
  green olives, sliced
4 eggs
black ground pepper

1 Heat oil in a large heavy pan, put in potatoes with 1 teaspoon salt. Stir to coat with oil and cook on moderate heat for about 10 minutes.
2 Stir in onion and cook for a further 10 minutes until potatoes are tender and becoming golden brown.
3 Turn mixture into a colander and drain off the oil and reserve.
4 Add olives to potatoes and onions.
5 In a large basin, whisk eggs with remaining salt and pepper until blended.
6 Add potato mixture to eggs.
7 Heat about 2 tablespoons of the reserved oil in a large frying pan, pour in omelette mixture and spread out evenly.
8 Allow to cook on moderate heat until set, and browned underneath.
9 Place a plate on top of pan, turn pan over so that omelette slips out onto plate.
10 Carefully slide omelette back into pan (browned side up) and cook for a further 2-3 minutes to brown underside.
11 Serve immediately, cut into 4.
Variations:
1 Peppers and tomatoes may be added, but are not traditionally Spanish.
2 Chopped fresh herbs are also nice but are not traditional.

Mushroom and Marmite soufflé

You will need for 3-4 servings:
METRIC/IMPERIAL
175 g/6 oz
  mushrooms
75 g/3 oz butter or
  margarine
50 g/2 oz plain flour
300 ml/½ pint milk

1 tablespoon Marmite
freshly ground pepper
¼ teaspoon dried
  thyme
4 large eggs

1 Wash and chop the mushrooms and cook for a few seconds in 25 g/1 oz of the butter or margarine.
2 Melt the remaining butter or margarine in a fairly large saucepan.
3 Stir in the flour, cook for 1 minute and gradually blend in the milk.
4 Remove pan from the heat and stir in the Marmite, mushrooms, ground pepper and thyme.

5 Separate the yolks from the whites and stir the yolks into the sauce.
6 Whisk the whites until stiff and dry and fold gently into the mixture in the pan.
7 Pour into a large, well greased soufflé dish and cook in a preheated moderately hot oven (190°C, 375°F, Gas Mark 5) on the centre shelf for 45-50 minutes until risen and firm to the touch.
8 Serve at once with a tossed salad.

Vegetable roulade

You will need for 4-6 servings:
METRIC/IMPERIAL
for the roulade:
65 g/2½ oz butter
25 g/1 oz flour
150 ml/¼ pint milk
50 g/2 oz Cheddar
  cheese, grated
5 standard eggs,
  separated
seasoning
25 g/1 oz Parmesan
  cheese
for the filling:
4 tablespoons olive oil

3 Spanish onions,
  sliced
2 cloves garlic,
  crushed
1 (397-g/14-oz) can
  tomatoes
¼ teaspoon dried
  thyme
1 teaspoon sugar
seasoning
25 g/1 oz stuffed
  green olives, sliced

1 First make the roulade. Using a 23-cm × 33-cm/9-inch × 13-inch Swiss roll tin, cut greaseproof paper 4 cm/1½ inches larger all round. Snip corners diagonally. Place on the greased tin and smooth paper flat. The corners will fold neatly into place. Oil the paper well.
2 Melt the butter in a pan, add the flour and cook for 1 minute.
3 Stir in the milk gradually and cook until thickened.
4 Add the Cheddar cheese. Remove pan from the heat, cool slightly.
5 Beat in the egg yolks, one or two at a time. Add the seasoning.
6 Whisk the egg whites until very stiff, then carefully fold into the cheese mixture.
7 Pour into the lined tin and spread evenly. Bake in a moderately hot oven (200°C, 400°F, Gas Mark 6) for 15 minutes on the upper shelf.
8 Sprinkle another sheet of paper with the Parmesan ready for the cooked roulade.
9 Meanwhile, make the filling. Place the oil in a frying pan, add the onions and garlic and fry until soft but not coloured.
10 Add the tomatoes, thyme, sugar, seasoning and olives.
11 Cook briskly without a lid, stirring from time to time, until the mixture is thick and pulpy.
12 Turn the cooked roulade onto the paper, remove the greaseproof paper and trim the edges.
13 Spread with ¾ of the filling and lift the paper to roll the roulade.
14 Put on the serving dish and pour the remaining filling over the top. Serve immediately.

Variations:

1 Make a mushroom filling using 50 g/2 oz butter and flour to 600 ml/1 pint milk to make a white sauce to which 350 g/12 oz sliced mushrooms and a little dried basil have been added.

2 Use 450 g/1 lb of Ratatouille (see page 15) to fill the roulade.

3 Fill with 450 g/1 lb chopped cooked spinach, seasoned and tossed in a little flour.

Curried vegetable pancakes

You will need for 4 servings:

METRIC/IMPERIAL

for the pancake batter:	1 clove garlic, crushed
100 g/4 oz plain flour	3 teaspoons curry powder
1 egg	300 ml/½ pint chicken stock
300 ml/½ pint milk	
seasoning	1 tablespoon tomato purée
oil or butter	
for the filling:	*for the sauce:*
225 g/8 oz carrots	15 g/½ oz butter
3 sticks celery	15 g/½ oz flour
1 large onion	300 ml/½ pint milk
1 green pepper	3 hard-boiled eggs
225 g/8 oz cauliflower florets	*to garnish:*
3 tablespoons oil	sprigs of watercress

1 Sift the flour into a bowl, add the egg and gradually add the milk, beating thoroughly to form a smooth batter. Season and allow to stand for at least 30 minutes.

2 Heat a little oil or butter in a frying pan and gradually pour in a little of the batter, tilting the pan to coat the base. Cook until golden brown, then turn and brown the other side. Repeat to make approximately 8 pancakes.

3 Peel and chop the carrots. Clean and slice the celery. Peel and chop the onion. Seed and chop the green pepper. Wash the cauliflower and break into small florets.

4 Heat the oil in a pan; add the carrots, celery, onion, green pepper and cauliflower. Cook, together with the garlic, until the onion and green pepper are soft.

5 Add the curry powder and cook, stirring continuously, for a few minutes.

6 Stir in the chicken stock and tomato purée. Season and simmer gently for 15-20 minutes, or until the vegetables are just soft and the liquid is reduced to a small amount of sauce. Use this mixture to fill the pancakes. Keep hot.

7 To make the sauce, melt the butter in a saucepan, stir in the flour and cook for a few minutes. Gradually stir in the milk and bring to the boil. Season.

8 Chop the hard-boiled eggs and stir into the sauce then pour over the pancakes and serve garnished with watercress.

Crunchy spinach pancakes

You will need for 4 servings:

METRIC/IMPERIAL

300 ml/½ pint pancake batter (see above)	*for the sauce:*
	50 g/2 oz butter
for the filling:	15 g/½ oz flour
100 g/4 oz walnuts, chopped	300 ml/½ pint dry white wine
450 g/1 lb cream cheese	½ chicken stock cube
1 large onion	1 tablespoon chopped parsley
50 g/2 oz butter	*to garnish:*
1 (227-g/8-oz) packet frozen chopped spinach	tomato wedges
	sprigs of parsley
100 g/4 oz button mushrooms, washed and sliced	
seasoning	

1 Make the pancakes (see above).

2 Mix together the walnuts and cream cheese and spread a little over each pancake.

3 Peel and chop the onion. Melt the butter in a pan, add the onion and cook until soft. Meanwhile, cook the spinach according to the instructions on the packet and drain thoroughly.

4 Add the spinach and mushrooms to the onion and mix. Season.

5 Cook the spinach mixture for 10 minutes then divide between the pancakes. Roll up and keep warm.

6 To make the sauce, melt the butter in a pan, add the flour and cook, stirring continuously, for a few minutes. Add the wine and stock cube. Bring to the boil, stirring continuously, and cook for a few minutes. Stir in the chopped parsley. Taste and adjust the seasoning if necessary.

7 Pour the sauce over the pancakes and serve garnished with tomato wedges and sprigs of parsley.

Sweetcorn and tomato pancakes

You will need for 4 servings:

METRIC/IMPERIAL

300 ml/½ pint pancake batter (see above)	*for the dressing:*
	100 g/4 oz streaky bacon
for the filling:	1 (150-g/5.3-oz) carton natural yoghurt
1 onion	
50 g/2 oz butter	
seasoning	1 tablespoon chopped mint
100 g/4 oz mushrooms	
	2 tablespoons double cream
1 (320-g/11½-oz) can sweetcorn	*to garnish:*
4 tomatoes	watercress

1 Make the pancakes (see above).

2 Peel and chop the onion. Melt the butter in a pan, add the onion and season. Cook until soft but not browned.

3 Clean and slice the mushrooms and add to the onion. Cook for a few minutes. Drain the sweetcorn and add to the onion mixture.

4 Skin the tomatoes and chop roughly. Add to the sweetcorn mixture and cook for a few minutes.

5 Fold the pancakes into quarters; then carefully fill the cone shape which is formed with the sweetcorn mixture. Arrange on a plate and keep warm.

6 Remove the rind from the bacon and chop finely. Cook over a gentle heat until fairly crisp, then mix with the yoghurt, mint and cream.

7 Garnish the pancakes with bunches of watercress and serve the dressing separately.

Pies, flans and pastries

Artichoke, ham and egg pie

You will need for 4 servings:

METRIC/IMPERIAL

450 g/1 lb knuckle of ham, soaked in water overnight	juice of ½ lemon
1 small carrot	1 kg/2 lb Jerusalem artichokes, cooked, peeled and sliced
1 celery stalk	4 hard-boiled eggs
4 cloves	100 g/4 oz Sage Derby
4 black peppercorns	or Cheddar cheese,
bouquet garni	grated
25 g/1 oz butter	few chopped sage
1 tablespoon flour	leaves
2 teaspoons dry mustard	350 g/12 oz flaky or puff pastry
300 ml/½ pint stock from boiling ham	beaten egg
2 tablespoons chopped parsley	

1 Drain ham. Place in a large pan and cover completely with cold water. Add carrot, celery, cloves, peppercorns and bouquet garni.

2 Bring to the boil and skim off any surface scum. Cover and simmer for 1 hour.

3 Lift out ham, remove rind and cool.

4 Strain stock and reserve. Dice ham.

5 Melt butter in a pan over low heat. Stir in flour and mustard and allow to bubble.

6 Gradually stir in stock to make a smooth sauce and simmer for 2 minutes. Stir in parsley and lemon juice. Fold in artichokes and ham.

7 Put about ⅓ of the mixture in the bottom of a large pie dish. Put an egg in each corner of the dish and spoon a little more of the artichoke and ham mixture in between the eggs.

8 Sprinkle with cheese and cover with the remaining artichoke and ham mixture. Sprinkle with the sage.

9 Cover with the pastry.

10 Brush with beaten egg. Bake in a moderately hot oven, (200°C, 400°F, Gas Mark 6) for 35 minutes or until the pastry is golden brown and puffy.

Mushroom and tomato flan

You will need for 3-4 servings:

METRIC/IMPERIAL

1 (20-cm/8-inch) baked pastry flan case	2 large tomatoes, skinned and chopped
for the filling:	3 teaspoons Marmite
100 g/4 oz mushrooms, chopped	2 large eggs
	150 ml/¼ pint milk

1 Place the flan case on a baking sheet.

2 Mix the mushrooms, tomatoes and Marmite together.

3 Beat the eggs well with the milk and stir into the vegetable mixture.

4 Pour into the flan case and bake on the centre shelf of a moderately hot oven (200°C, 400°F, Gas Mark 6) for 40 minutes.

Leek and cheese flan

You will need for 4 servings:

METRIC/IMPERIAL

1 (213-g/7½-oz) packet frozen shortcrust pastry, thawed	2 egg yolks
1 kg/2 lb medium leeks	50 g/2 oz grated cheese
1 (142-ml/5-fl oz) carton soured cream	seasoning

1 Roll out the pastry on a lightly floured board and use to line a shallow 18-cm/7-inch square tin.

2 Lightly prick the base and line with greaseproof paper and baking beans kept for the purpose.

3 Bake on the centre shelf of a moderately hot oven (200°C, 400°F, Gas Mark 6) for 15 minutes.

4 Remove the paper and baking beans and cook for a further 10 minutes to cook the centre of the pastry.

5 Remove the flan and reduce the oven temperature to moderate (180°C, 350°F, Gas Mark 4).

6 Meanwhile, trim the leeks, removing the green leaves (reserve these for soup).

7 Wash the leeks very thoroughly to remove any grit.

8 Bring a pan of salted water to the boil and cook the leeks gently for about 10 minutes or until just tender, depending on thickness. Test with a skewer.

9 Remove the leeks and drain very well by placing on kitchen paper.

10 Arrange the leeks in the base of the flan, cutting to fit if necessary.

11 Mix the soured cream, egg yolks and cheese together. Add the seasoning.

12 Spoon this mixture evenly over the leeks and cook in the centre of the oven for 20 minutes, until the mixture is set when lightly pressed with the fingers.

Variations:

1 Make your own pastry using 100 g/4 oz wholemeal flour.

2 Add 1 tablespoon of real mayonnaise and 1 teaspoon dried thyme to the eggs and soured cream.

Spinach flan

You will need for 4-5 servings:

METRIC/IMPERIAL

175 g/6 oz plain 81% stone ground flour	1 (225-g/8-oz) packet finely chopped frozen spinach
salt	
75 g/3 oz margarine	1 teaspoon yeast extract
2 tablespoons water	
for the filling:	2 tablespoons flour
50 g/2 oz margarine	3 large eggs
375 g/12 oz onions, sliced	175 g/6 oz Cheddar cheese, grated
1 clove garlic, crushed	salt and pepper

1 Place the flour and salt in a bowl and rub in the margarine until mixture resembles fine breadcrumbs.

2 Add the water quickly, mixing lightly to form a dough. Put in a polythene bag and rest the pastry in a cool place for about 30 minutes.

3 Meanwhile, make the filling. Melt the margarine, add the onions, garlic and spinach, cover and cook over a low heat for 30 minutes, stirring occasionally to prevent the mixture sticking. Stir in the yeast extract.

4 Stir in the flour, cook for 2 minutes and remove from the heat.

5 Beat the eggs well and add to the pan with 100 g/4 oz of the cheese, salt and pepper.

6 Roll out the pastry between two sheets of greaseproof paper. Use to line a 26-cm/10-inch fluted flan dish.

7 Add the filling and place on the centre shelf in a moderately hot oven (190°C, 375°F, Gas Mark 5) and cook for 25 minutes.

8 Sprinkle on remaining cheese in lines and return to the oven for a further 5-7 minutes to just melt the cheese.

9 Serve with a colourful salad and French bread.

Tomato and olive quiche

You will need for 8 servings:

METRIC/IMPERIAL

375 g/12 oz shortcrust pastry	3 large eggs
for the filling:	50 g/2 oz stuffed olives, halved
2 tablespoons olive oil	75 g/3 oz grated cheese
1 medium-sized onion, chopped	seasoning
450 g/1 lb tomatoes, skinned and sliced	2 tablespoons tomato purée
1 teaspoon dried oregano or marjoram	

1 Roll out the pastry and use to line a 23-cm/9-inch fluted flan tin. Lightly prick the base.

2 Heat the oil and cook the onion to lightly brown.

3 Add the tomatoes and herbs.

4 Beat the eggs and add with the olives, half the cheese, seasoning.

5 Cook for 5 minutes then cool a little.

6 Spread the tomato purée in the base of the flan.

7 Pour in the cooled mixture.

8 Sprinkle with the remaining cheese.

9 Cook in a moderately hot oven (190°C, 375°F, Gas Mark 5) for 45 minutes.

10 Serve hot or cold.

Variations:

1 Make wholemeal pastry for the base.

2 Fry green pepper with the onion; omit the olives.

Flan niçoise

You will need for 4 servings:

METRIC/IMPERIAL

1 (198-g/7-oz) packet shortcrust pastry	seasoning
1 tablespoon oil	8 stuffed green olives, sliced
large onion, chopped	50 g/2 oz anchovies
2 eggs	
150 g/¼ pint single cream	

1 Roll out pastry and use to line an 18-cm/7-inch flan tin; lightly prick the base.

2 Chill for 15 minutes to relax the pastry.

3 Fill the flan case with greaseproof paper and beans, or crumpled foil.

4 Bake blind in a hot oven (220°C, 425°F, Gas Mark 7) for about 10 minutes until beginning to brown lightly at the edges.

5 Remove beans or foil and dry out for further 5 minutes.

6 While the flan case is cooking, prepare the filling. Heat the oil and fry the onion until pale brown and cooked through, about 10 minutes.

7 Remove from the heat, cool slightly and then spread evenly over the base of the flan.

8 Whisk eggs with a fork, add cream and seasoning and pour into the flan.

9 Sprinkle with most of the sliced olives and arrange a lattice of anchovies over the top. This will sink a bit but this doesn't matter.

10 Return to a moderate oven (180°C, 350°F, Gas Mark 4) for about 20 minutes until set.

11 Decorate with a few more sliced olives.

Asparagus quiche

You will need for 4-6 helpings:
METRIC/IMPERIAL

175 g/6 oz shortcrust pastry	15 g/½ oz butter
350 g/12 oz fresh, thin asparagus spears	2 large eggs
6 spring onions, washed and trimmed	150 ml/¼ pint thin cream
	seasoning

1 Line an 18-cm/7-inch flan dish or ring with pastry.

2 Blanch asparagus for 5 minutes. Drain and allow to cool. Slice onions and cook gently in the butter until soft.

3 Whisk the eggs with the cream, salt and pepper and add to the onions. Cut the asparagus into 2.5-cm/1-inch lengths and stir into the mixture.

4 Pour into prepared flan case and spread out the asparagus if necessary.

5 Bake in a preheated moderately hot oven (200°C, 400°F, Gas Mark 6) for 15 minutes. Reduce the heat to moderate (180°C, 350°F, Gas Mark 4) and bake for a further 20 minutes or until the centre is cooked.

Pissaladière

You will need for 4-5 servings:
METRIC/IMPERIAL

for the base:	4 tablespoons oil
225 g/8 oz self-raising flour	225 g/8 oz tomatoes, skinned and sliced
½ level teaspoon salt	black pepper
25 g/1 oz butter or margarine	4 slices Mozzarella cheese
150 ml/¼ pint milk	50 g/2 oz anchovies, cut into strips
for the topping:	20 stuffed green olives
3 medium-sized onions	

1 Put flour and salt in a bowl, rub in the butter or margarine. Mix with the milk to a firm dough.

2 Roll out on a lightly floured surface to a 23-cm/9-inch circle.

3 Place on a baking sheet, and, using the thumb and forefinger, raise the edge slightly by pinching the dough.

4 Slice the onions and fry in the oil to soften without colouring, about 10 minutes.

5 Spread the onions on top of the dough, cover with tomato slices, sprinkle with pepper and top with cheese slices.

6 Bake in a hot oven (220°C, 425°F, Gas Mark 7) for about 20 minutes. Lay strips of anchovy on top and decorate with olives. Cook for a further 10 minutes until the dough is browned.

7 Serve hot with a green salad.

Pizza pie

You will need for 4 servings:
METRIC/IMPERIAL

225 g/8 oz wholemeal flour	75 g/3 oz grated cheese
2 teaspoons baking powder	75 g/3 oz sunflower seeds (optional)
seasoning	2 tomatoes, skinned and sliced
75 g/3 oz margarine, cut into pieces	*to garnish:*
150 ml/¼ pint milk	2 tablespoons chopped parsley or oregano or marjoram
2 rashers streaky bacon	
1 large onion	1 tablespoon grated Parmesan cheese
1 large red pepper	
225 g/8 oz mushrooms	
2 tablespoons oil	
1 clove garlic, crushed	
1 tablespoon basil	
2 tablespoons chopped parsley	
1 (397-g/14-oz) can tomatoes	

1 Mix together the flour and baking powder. Season with salt and pepper, then rub in the margarine. Mix to a soft dough with the milk.

2 Knead lightly, then roll out to line a 26-cm/10-inch quiche dish.

3 Remove the rind from the bacon and chop; peel and slice the onion; remove the seeds from the pepper and slice; clean and slice the mushrooms.

4 Heat the oil in a pan, add the garlic, bacon, onion and pepper. Season and cook stirring continuously, until the onion is just soft.

5 Add the herbs, mushrooms, can of tomatoes and cheese, then turn into the lined quiche dish.

6 Grease a heavy-based pan with little oil, then add the sunflower seeds and sauté, stirring continuously for a few minutes.

7 Arrange the tomatoes around the edge of the pie and sprinkle the sunflower seeds in the centre. Brush the edge of the pastry with oil.

8 Bake in a preheated hot oven (220°C, 425°F, Gas Mark 7) for 15 minutes; then reduce the temperature to moderately hot (180°C, 375°F, Gas Mark 5) and cook for a further 20-25 minutes.

9 Mix together the chopped parsley and Parmesan and sprinkle over the pie before serving.

Angela's spinach vol-au-vent

You will need for 4 servings:

METRIC/IMPERIAL

350 g/12 oz flaky
  pastry mix
beaten egg or milk
for the filling:
50 g/2 oz butter or
  margarine
2 medium onions,
  finely chopped
1 (225-g/8-oz) packet
  frozen spinach
1 small clove garlic,
  crushed
2 tablespoons flour
150 ml/¼ pint milk
seasoning
¼ teaspoon dried
  mixed herbs

3 hard-boiled eggs,
  coarsely chopped
50 g/2 oz flaked
  almonds

1 Make up the pastry mix according to the packet directions.
2 Divide the pastry in half, and roll out each on a floured board to an oblong 24 × 18 cm/9½ × 7 inches.
3 Cut each into an oval 22 × 14 cm/8½ × 6 inches, using a 500-ml/l-pint oval pie dish as a guide.
4 Place one oval on a lightly dampened baking sheet and brush the edge lightly with water.
5 Lightly score the second oval all over in a diamond pattern using a sharp knife; then mark the pastry 2-cm/1-inch from the edge and cut out the centre oval.
6 Carefully lift the pastry rim on top of the first oval and press down. Knock up edges with the back of a knife.
7 Place the smaller piece on a baking sheet.
8 Brush lightly with beaten egg or milk.
9 Bake on an upper centre shelf of a hot oven (220°C, 425°F, Gas Mark 7) for 15-20 minutes, until risen and golden brown.
10 Remove from the oven and keep hot.
11 Meanwhile, make the filling. Melt the butter or margarine in a heavy based saucepan, preferably non-stick.
12 Add the onions and frozen spinach. Cook over a very gentle heat, turning the spinach to aid thawing, about 12-15 minutes. (This is done slowly as the juice from the spinach is required for the sauce).
13 Add the garlic and flour to the pan, cook for 2 minutes.
14 Gradually add the milk, bring to the boil, stirring, and cook for 2 minutes.
15 Season well with salt and pepper and add the herbs.
16 Stir in the eggs and flaked almonds.
17 Pour into the vol-au-vent case, put the lid on and serve at once.
18 Serve with a salad and sauté potatoes.

Variation:

Use sweetcorn kernels instead of spinach.

Piquant vol-au-vent

You will need for 4 servings:

METRIC/IMPERIAL

1 (400-g/14-oz) packet
  puff pastry
little beaten egg
for the filling:
4 rashers streaky
  bacon, chopped
100 g/4 oz button
  mushrooms, sliced

25 g/1 oz butter
25 g/1 oz flour
300 ml/½ pint milk
25 g/1 oz stuffed
  green olives, sliced
seasoning

1 Roll out pastry on a floured surface to a square about 15 × 15 cm/6 × 6 inches.
2 With a sharp pointed knife, 2 cm/1 inch in from the outside mark a 10-cm/4-inch square within the outer square, cutting down almost to the base of the pastry.
3 Flute edges and glaze with beaten egg.
4 Bake in a very hot oven (230°C, 450°F, Gas Mark 8) for about 15-20 minutes, until well risen and brown.
5 Take off the lid and scoop out the moist pastry centre.
6 Lower the oven temperature to moderately hot (200°C, 400°F, Gas Mark 6) and dry out the pastry case for about 10 minutes.
7 Meanwhile, make the filling. Put the bacon in a pan on a low heat to draw out the fat.
8 Then fry gently until pale golden. Add mushrooms and cook quickly for 1 minute, stirring all the time.
9 Lift out the bacon and mushrooms on to a plate with a slotted spoon.
10 Add butter to the pan, then flour, and make a white sauce with the milk. Cook for 2 minutes.
11 Add reserved bacon and mushrooms and the olives. Season, then pour into the pastry case and serve at once.

Spinach plait

You will need for 4-6 servings:

METRIC/IMPERIAL

225 g/8 oz flour
seasoning
1 teaspoon dried
  mixed herbs
100 g/4 oz margarine
cold water to mix
1 large onion
100 g/4 oz streaky
  bacon
100 g/4 oz
  mushrooms,
  washed

50 g/2 oz butter
2 (227-g/8-oz) packets
  frozen chopped
  spinach
little milk to glaze
to serve:
cheese sauce
  seasoned with
  nutmeg

1 Sieve the flour into a bowl with the seasoning and herbs. Add the margarine, cut into pieces and rub in lightly with the fingertips. Mix with sufficient cold water to bind the pastry.

2 Roll out the pastry to make a rectangle of 27 × 30 cm/11 × 12 inches. Place the pastry on a baking sheet.

3 Peel and chop the onion, remove the rind from the bacon and chop, then dice the mushrooms.

4 Melt the butter in the pan, add the onion and bacon and cook until soft. Add the mushrooms and cook for a few minutes.

5 Cook the spinach according to the instructions on the packet, then add to the onion and bacon mixture. Season and place in a neat heap down the centre of the pastry.

6 Make slanting cuts in the pastry towards the spinach mixture to give strips of pastry approximately 3 cm/1½ inches in width. Brush the strips with water and plait over the spinach filling.

7 Brush the plait with a little milk and bake in a moderately hot oven (200°C, 400°F, Gas Mark 6) for 35-40 minutes or until the pastry is cooked and golden.

8 Serve with a cheese sauce seasoned with a little grated nutmeg.

Vegetable pasties

You will need for 4 servings:
METRIC/IMPERIAL
350 g/12 oz plain flour
pinch salt
175 g/6 oz margarine
cold water to mix
for the filling:
1 tablespoon oil
3 tablespoons
    sunflower seeds
1 clove garlic, crushed
1 teaspoon dried
    mixed herbs
1 tablespoon chopped
    parsley
225 g/8 oz leeks,
    washed and sliced
1 large carrot,
    chopped
100 g/4 oz
    mushrooms, sliced
to glaze:
beaten egg or milk

1 Sift the flour into a bowl with the salt. Add the margarine and rub into the flour until the mixture resembles fine breadcrumbs.

2 Mix to a firm dough using a little water. Divide into four.

3 Heat the oil in a pan, add the sunflower seeds and cook for a few minutes. Add the garlic, herbs and remaining ingredients. Cook for a few minutes then cool.

4 Roll out each piece of pastry to a circle approximately 20 cm/8 inches in diameter. Divide the filling among the circles, dampen the edges, seal to enclose the filling and crimp the edges.

5 Brush with beaten egg or milk and bake in a moderately hot oven (200°C, 400°F, Gas Mark 6) for 35-40 minutes.

6 Cool for a few minutes on a wire rack and serve while hot.
Variation:
Use wholemeal flour.

Rice dishes

Giralda rice

You will need for 8 servings:
METRIC/IMPERIAL
1 medium-sized
    aubergine
8 tablespoons oil
5 large tomatoes,
    peeled
2 cloves garlic,
    crushed
1 medium-sized
    onion, chopped
225 g/8 oz long-grain
    rice, washed
225 g/8 oz green
    peppers, seeds
    removed
600 ml/1 pint chicken
    stock
150 ml/¼ pint dry
    white wine
pinch saffron
225 g/8 oz peeled
    prawns
225 g/8 oz frozen
    cockles (optional)
75 g/3 oz Spanish
    stuffed green
    olives, sliced
75 g/3 oz Gruyère
    cheese, grated

1 Slice unpeeled aubergine in 1-cm/½-inch slices, sprinkle with salt and stand for 30 minutes. Rinse, drain and dry.

2 Sauté in four tablespoons of the oil until lightly browned and tender. Drain on kitchen paper.

3 Slice two tomatoes and keep on one side.

4 Chop the remainder and put into a large pan with the remaining oil, garlic, onion and rice. Cook, stirring constantly for 2-3 minutes.

5 Add peppers, stock, wine and saffron, stir well and simmer for about 15 minutes, until rice is just tender and liquid absorbed.

6 Stir in shellfish and olives; cook for further 5 minutes.

7 Turn into a paella pan, or large shallow serving dish. Arrange tomatoes and aubergine slices alternately round edge. Sprinkle with cheese and grill until lightly browned.

8 Serve very hot, with green salad.
Variation:
Use a jar of mussels, well drained.

Summer risotto

You will need for 4 servings:

METRIC/IMPERIAL

50 g/2 oz margarine	2 tablespoons corn oil
1 large onion, chopped	1 tablespoon white wine vinegar
100 g/4 oz button mushrooms, sliced	100 g/4 oz cold cooked peas
175 g/6 oz long-grain rice	1 (198-g/7-oz) can sweetcorn with peppers
1 teaspoon Marmite dissolved in 600-750 ml/1-1¼ pints boiling water	175 g/6 oz Gouda cheese, cut into small dice
pinch each salt, pepper, dry mustard and castor sugar	50 g/2 oz sultanas (optional)

1 Melt the margarine in a large frying pan, add the onion and cook gently for 5 minutes.
2 Stir in the mushrooms, cook for a few seconds, stir in the rice and cook for 1 minute.
3 Add 600 ml/1 pint of the Marmite stock.
4 Cook gently with lid on for 20-25 minutes until the rice is just tender and has absorbed the stock.
5 Add the extra stock if necessary.
6 Remove from the heat and allow to cool.
7 To make the dressing, place salt, pepper, mustard and sugar in a serving bowl, blend in the oil gradually, and beat in the vinegar.
8 Add the cooked rice and remaining ingredients, stir and serve at once with a green salad.

Chinese pilaff

You will need for 4-6 servings:

METRIC/IMPERIAL

450 g/1 lb brown rice	1 small red pepper, seeded and thinly sliced
3 teaspoons Marmite	
25 g/1 oz margarine	225 g/8 oz carrots, thinly sliced
225 g/8 oz onions, sliced	
½ teaspoon dried mixed herbs	225 g/8 oz bean shoots
1 small green pepper, seeded and thinly sliced	50 g/2 oz peanuts
	2 tablespoons chopped parsley

1 Wash rice thoroughly, put into a large saucepan of water and bring to the boil. Add 2 teaspoons of the Marmite, blend in carefully, reduce heat, cover with lid and simmer without stirring for 40-45 minutes.
2 Meanwhile, melt margarine in large saucepan, add onions and mixed herbs, cover and cook for 5 minutes.
3 Stir in peppers and sauté for 5 minutes.
4 Pour in 300 ml/½ pint cold water, stir well, add carrots and dissolve remaining teaspoon Marmite in the water.

5 Cook for further 5 minutes, finally add bean shoots, stir gently from time to time and cook until just tender, about 5 minutes.
6 Drain the rice well, return to pan and stir in the peanuts and chopped parsley. Arrange in the centre of a heated serving dish and arrange vegetables on each side.

Variation:
Add ½ teaspoon chopped fresh thyme and ¼ teaspoon fresh marjoram instead of the dried mixed herbs.

Note:
A little grated Parmesan sprinkled over each serving, although not Chinese, is very tasty.

Cauliflower and rice suprême

You will need for 4 servings:

METRIC/IMPERIAL

100 g/4 oz brown rice	40 g/1½ oz plain flour
2 teaspoons salt	pepper
1 medium-sized cauliflower	2 eggs, well beaten
175 g/6 oz onions, chopped	50 g/2 oz Cheddar cheese, grated
¼ teaspoon each dried sage and mixed herbs	to garnish:
	1 punnet mustard and cress, trimmed and washed
40 g/1½ oz butter or margarine	

1 Soak rice in cold water for 30 minutes; drain well.
2 Put rice in a heavy based saucepan, cover with 300 ml/½ pint water and 1 teaspoon of the salt.
3 Bring to the boil, reduce heat, simmer for 35-40 minutes until tender.
4 Prepare cauliflower by removing coarse outside stalks and washing it. Remove centre stalk and chop it.
5 Divide cauliflower into florets.
6 Put onions and cauliflower into saucepan, add 250 ml/8 fl oz cold water and remaining salt, cover with a tight fitting lid and bring to the boil. Cook for 8 minutes.
7 Add sage and mixed herbs; cook for a further 2 minutes. (Cauliflower should be tender but not soft.)
8 Drain the cauliflower, reserving the liquor to give 250 ml/8 fl oz: add extra water if necessary. Keep cauliflower on one side.
9 Melt butter or margarine in a saucepan, stir in the flour and cook for 1 minute.
10 Gradually add the reserved liquor, stirring well to remove any lumps. Bring to the boil and cook for 2 minutes.
11 Stir in the cauliflower and adjust seasoning.
12 Strain any excess water from the rice and add to the cauliflower mixture, stirring in gently.
13 Stir in the beaten eggs and cheese.
14 Thoroughly butter a 1-litre/2-pint ring mould and press in the mixture.

15 Cook in a preheated moderate oven (180°C, 350°F, Gas Mark 4) on the centre shelf until firm to the touch (about 20 minutes).

16 Loosen the edges with a knife, place a plate on top and very carefully turn out.

17 Fill the centre with the mustard and cress. Serve with a tomato and cucumber salad.

Variations:

1 If liked, serve with a fresh tomato sauce (see page 85).

2 If cauliflower is not available this recipe could be done with ½ kg/1¼ lbs prepared leeks finely chopped and cooked in the same way as the cauliflower. Fill the centre with 225 g/8 oz cooked runner beans.

Provençal rice

You will need for 4 servings:

METRIC/IMPERIAL
2 tablespoons
  vegetable oil
225 g/8 oz courgettes,
  sliced
1 red pepper, chopped
1 yellow pepper,
  chopped
4 tomatoes, peeled
  and quartered
2 medium-sized
  onions, sliced
seasoning
marjoram
225 g/8 oz long-grain
  rice
600 ml/1 pint stock
1 sprig fresh thyme
1 bay leaf
2 cloves garlic,
  crushed
175 g/6 oz French
  beans, sliced,
  poached for 5
  minutes
75 g/3 oz grated ,
  Gruyère cheese
  (optional)

1 Heat the oil in a pan.

2 Mix together the courgettes, peppers, tomatoes and onions and place in the oil.

3 Fry the mixture over a high heat for 5 minutes, stirring continuously.

4 Season with salt, pepper and marjoram.

5 Reduce heat and simmer for 5 minutes, stirring occasionally.

6 Add the rice and cook for 2-3 minutes before adding the stock, thyme, bay leaf, crushed garlic and beans.

7 Bring to the boil and stir once.

8 Lower heat to simmer, cover and cook for 15 minutes or until rice is tender and liquid absorbed.

9 Serve with the grated cheese as desired.

Red cabbage risotto

You will need for 4 servings:

METRIC/IMPERIAL
1 medium-sized onion
25 g/1 oz butter
3 tablespoons oil
100 g/4 oz easy-cook
  rice
1 chicken stock cube
300 ml/½ pint boiling
  water
125 g/4 oz streaky
  bacon

1 large green pepper
350 g/12 oz red
  cabbage
2 teaspoons caraway
  seeds or celery seed
1 clove garlic, crushed
100 g/4 oz
  mushrooms
freshly ground black
  pepper

1 Peel and thinly slice the onion.

2 Heat the butter in a pan together with 1 tablespoon of the oil. Add the rice and cook, stirring continuously, until browned. Stir in the onion.

3 Add the stock cube and water, stir until dissolved, then cover and simmer gently until all the liquid has been absorbed. Remove pan from the heat.

4 Meanwhile, remove the rind from the bacon and chop. Shred the green pepper and cabbage.

5 Heat the remaining oil in a pan, add the caraway seeds and garlic. Cook for a few minutes.

6 Add the bacon and green pepper, then cook until the bacon is cooked and the green pepper just soft.

7 Add the cabbage and cook, stirring occasionally, for 10 minutes or until the cabbage is slightly softened.

8 Finally, stir in the sliced mushrooms and cooked rice. Cook for a few minutes, season with pepper and serve immediately.

Pasta dishes

Tomato bolognaise

You will need for 4-5 servings:

METRIC/IMPERIAL
1 large onion,
  chopped
1 tablespoon corn oil
675 g/1½ lb tomatoes,
  chopped
3 teaspoons Marmite
1 tablespoon
  cornflour
pepper

1 tablespoon tomato
  purée
2 teaspoons sugar
225 g/8 oz spaghetti
  or noodles
to garnish:
Parmesan cheese
  (optional)

1 Place the onion in a saucepan with the oil and cook for 5 minutes to soften the onion.

2 Add the tomatoes and cook steadily for 30 minutes to reduce the liquid a little. Stir in the Marmite.

3 Blend the cornflour with a little water, then pour on some of the hot liquid, stir and add to the pan.

4 Bring to the boil and cook until sauce thickens and clears. Add the pepper to taste, sugar and tomato purée.

5 Meanwhile, cook the spaghetti or noodles in boiling salted water until tender, about 10-15 minutes. Drain well and serve with the sauce on top.

6 If liked, serve with grated Parmesan cheese.

Variations:

1 Add a crushed clove of garlic to the onion.

2 Add fresh or dried herbs, basil, marjoram or oregano.

3 Quartered stuffed olives or stoned black olives add extra piquancy to the sauce.

Savoury mushroom spaghetti

You will need for 2 servings:

METRIC/IMPERIAL

100 g/4 oz spaghetti	225 g/8 oz button
3 tablespoons oil	mushrooms, sliced
2 onions, thinly sliced	5 anchovy fillets
2 cloves garlic,	6 stuffed olives, sliced
crushed	*to serve:*
3 rashers back bacon,	Parmesan cheese
chopped	

1 Cook the spaghetti in boiling salted water for about 12 minutes until tender.

2 Meanwhile, place the oil in a saucepan with the onions, and cook for 5 minutes.

3 Add the garlic and bacon and cook gently for 5 minutes.

4 Add the mushrooms, anchovies and olives; heat through slowly.

5 Drain the spaghetti, serve with the sauce on top, sprinkled with the Parmesan cheese.

Variation:

Use 2 large tomatoes, chopped, instead of the anchovies.

Wholemeal spaghetti with mushrooms and leeks

You will need for 4 servings:

METRIC/IMPERIAL

2 medium-sized leeks	150 ml/¼ pint double
225 g/8 oz button	cream
mushrooms	seasoning
225 g/8 oz wholemeal	*to garnish:*
spaghetti	chopped parsley or
50 g/2 oz butter	fresh herbs
1 clove garlic	
(optional)	

1 Wash the leeks and slice thinly, then rewash to remove any remaining grit. Drain thoroughly.

2 Wipe the mushrooms and slice thinly.

3 Cook the spaghetti in plenty of boiling salted water until tender (about 12 minutes).

4 Meanwhile, melt the butter in a pan, then add the crushed clove of garlic, if used, and leeks.

5 Cook, stirring continuously, until the leeks are soft but not browned.

6 Stir in the mushrooms, cook and continue stirring for a few minutes.

7 Stir in the cream, season and heat through but do not allow to boil.

8 Drain the spaghetti, place in a warmed serving dish and pour over the leeks and mushrooms.

9 Toss well and sprinkle with chopped parsley before serving immediately.

Vegetable lasagne

You will need for 4-5 servings:

METRIC/IMPERIAL

175 g/6 oz lasagne	*for the sauce:*
1 teaspoon corn oil	50 g/2 oz margarine
for the vegetable	50 g/2 oz flour
filling:	450 ml/¾ pint milk
50 g/2 oz margarine	¼ teaspoon made
225 g/8 oz onions,	mustard
chopped	75 g/3 oz grated
225 g/8 oz leeks,	Cheddar cheese
trimmed and	and 75 g/3 oz grated
washed	Gruyère cheese
1 (397-g/14-oz) can	mixed together
peeled tomatoes	seasoning
225 g/8 oz	
mushrooms,	
washed and	
coarsely chopped	
½ teaspoon dried	
mixed herbs	
1 teaspoon Marmite	
seasoning	

1 Cook the lasagne in plenty of boiling salted water with the oil, making sure they do not stick together, and cook until just tender, about 13 minutes or according to the instructions on the packet.

2 Drain and separate the lasagne, leave on one side.

3 To make the filling, melt the margarine, add the onions and cook for 5 minutes without browning.

4 Finely chop leeks and add with the tomatoes, cover and cook for 5 minutes.

5 Add the mushrooms, herbs, Marmite, seasoning, stir to dissolve Marmite, cover and cook gently for 10 minutes.

6 To make the sauce, melt the margarine, add the flour and cook for 1 minute. Gradually stir in the milk, bring to the boil, stirring, and cook for 2 minutes.

7 Stir in the mustard and 125 g/4 oz of the cheese, add seasoning to taste and cook for 1 minute.

8 In a large ovenproof dish, arrange layers of the pasta, vegetables and sauce alternately, ending with a layer of sauce.

9 Sprinkle with remaining cheese and cook in a pre-heated moderate oven (180°C, 350°F, Gas Mark 4) for 20-25 minutes.

10 Serve with a green salad and French bread.

Tomato and leek lasagne

You will need for 4-6 servings:

METRIC/IMPERIAL

225 g/8 oz lasagne	*for the sauce:*
175 g/6 oz streaky	15 g/½ oz butter
bacon	15 g/½ oz flour
6 leeks	300 ml/½ pint milk
450 g/1 lb tomatoes	75 g/3 oz Cheddar
2 tablespoons oil	cheese, grated
2 cloves garlic,	chopped parsley
crushed	
2 teaspoons dried	
sweet basil	
seasoning	

1 Cook the lasagne in boiling salted water until tender, according to the packet directions.
2 Drain, rinse and dry on kitchen paper.
3 Remove the rind from the bacon and chop.
4 Wash the leeks and slice; re-wash to remove all the grit.
5 Skin the tomatoes and chop. Heat the oil in a pan, add the bacon, garlic and leeks.
6 Cook, stirring continuously, until the leeks are soft.
7 Add the tomatoes and basil, season and cook for 4-5 minutes.
8 Melt the butter in a saucepan, add the flour and cook for a few minutes.
9 Gradually stir in the milk and bring to the boil, stirring continuously.
10 Add 50 g/2 oz of the cheese and cook, stirring, until it has melted. Season to taste.
11 Layer the lasagne with the leek and tomato mixture in an ovenproof dish.
12 Pour the sauce over the top and sprinkle with the remaining grated cheese.
13 Bake in a moderately hot preheated oven (190°C, 375°F, Gas Mark 5) for approximately 30 minutes until golden brown. Sprinkle with parsley and serve immediately with a tossed salad.

Vegetable cannelloni

You will need for 3-4 servings:

METRIC/IMPERIAL

1 medium-sized onion	25 g/1 oz Parmesan
2 tablespoons corn oil	cheese, grated
1 (397-g/14-oz) can	seasoning
peeled tomatoes	1 (25-g/1-oz) packet
2 teaspoons Marmite	savoury white or
175 g/6 oz frozen	onion sauce mix
chopped spinach,	10 uncooked tubes
thawed	cannelloni
1 egg, well beaten	300 ml/½ pint milk
50 g/2 oz brown	extra cheese
breadcrumbs	(optional)

1 Chop the onion and place in a saucepan with the oil; cook for 5 minutes without browning.
2 Add the tomatoes and Marmite, stir, and cook gently for 5 minutes.

3 Take out 6 tablespoons of the mixture and place in a bowl.
4 Spread the remainder in an ovenproof dish just large enough to take the cannelloni in a single layer.
5 Squeeze the water out of the spinach, add to the tomato in the bowl with the egg, breadcrumbs, Parmesan and seasoning.
6 Using a small spoon or knife, stuff this mixture into the cannelloni and arrange in the dish.
7 Make up the sauce with the milk according to the directions on the packet and pour evenly over the cannelloni to completely cover.
8 Sprinkle with a little extra cheese if liked.
9 Bake in the centre of a moderately hot oven (200°C, 400°F, Gas Mark 6) for 30 minutes.
10 Serve with a tossed green salad.

Mushroom cannelloni

You will need for 4 servings:

METRIC/IMPERIAL

1 onion	150 ml/¼ pint dry red
25 g/1 oz butter	wine
225 g/8 oz button	2 tablespoons
mushrooms	redcurrant jelly
50 g/2 oz liver	1 tablespoon tomato
sausage	purée
100 g/4 oz cream	2 teaspoons cornflour
cheese	*to garnish:*
seasoning	sprigs of watercress
8 tubes cannelloni	tomato slices

1 Peel and chop the onion. Melt the butter in a pan, add the onion and cook over a gentle heat until soft but not browned.
2 Wipe or wash the mushrooms and chop finely. Dice the liver sausage and mix with the mushrooms, cream cheese and onion. Season.
3 Cook the cannelloni in boiling salted water until tender. Drain and rinse in cold water, then drain well on kitchen paper.
4 Using a teaspoon, stuff the cannelloni with the mushroom mixture and arrange in a buttered ovenproof dish.
5 Heat the wine, redcurrant jelly and tomato purée together in a saucepan until the jelly has dissolved. Blend the cornflour with a little cold water until smooth, stir into the wine mixture and bring to the boil, stirring continuously.
6 Pour the sauce over the cannelloni, cover with foil and bake in a preheated moderate oven (180°C, 350°F, Gas Mark 4) for 20 minutes.
7 Serve garnished with sprigs of watercress and slices of tomato.

Variation:
The cannelloni may be served with a creamy sauce using 15 g/½ oz butter, 15 g/½ oz flour and 300 ml/½ pint milk. Sprinkle with 50 g/2 oz grated cheese and bake, uncovered, in a preheated moderate oven (180°C, 350°F, Gas Mark 4) for 30 minutes.

Savoury vegetable macaroni cheese

You will need for 4 servings:

METRIC/IMPERIAL

225 g/8 oz macaroni
225 g/8 oz frozen
   mixed vegetables
3 large tomatoes
50 g/2 oz butter or
   margarine
50 g/2 oz plain flour
600 ml/1 pint milk
1 teaspoon dried
   mixed herbs
   (optional)

3 teaspoons Marmite
175 g/6 oz Cheddar
   cheese, grated

1 Cook macaroni in plenty of boiling salted water for 10 minutes until tender. Drain well.
2 Thaw the vegetables and skin and chop the tomatoes.
3 Melt the butter or margarine, stir in the flour and gradually add the milk. Bring to the boil, stirring, and cook for 2 minutes. Add the vegetables, tomatoes, herbs, if used, Marmite and half the cheese to the macaroni.
4 Pour into a buttered 1.25-litre/2-pint ovenproof dish, sprinkle over the remaining cheese and cook on the centre shelf of a moderately hot oven (200°C, 400°F, Gas Mark 6) for 20 minutes.

Pasta with avocado and lemon sauce

You will need for 4 servings:

METRIC/IMPERIAL

225 g/8 oz large pasta
   shells, or other
   short cut pasta
5 tablespoons French
   dressing (see page
   86)
1 large ripe avocado
juice and grated rind
   of 1 lemon
seasoning
1 clove garlic, crushed

2 teaspoons sugar
3-4 tablespoons stock
   or milk
4 spring onions,
   chopped
2 tablespoons
   chopped parsley

1 Cook pasta shells in boiling salted water until just tender. Drain well and toss lightly in French dressing while still warm.
2 Halve the avocado, remove the stone and scoop out the flesh.
3 Put into an electric blender and blend until smooth with the lemon juice, seasoning, garlic, sugar and stock.
4 Stir in the spring onions and parsley; the sauce may be thinned with extra stock or milk if liked.
5 Stir the avocado and lemon sauce into the pasta.
6 Serve cold, with tomato salad.

Vegetable Accompaniments

Casserole of artichokes and mushrooms

You will need for 4 servings:

METRIC/IMPERIAL

450 g/1 lb Jerusalem
   artichokes
50 g/2 oz butter
225 g/8 oz small
   button mushrooms,
   washed
25 g/1 oz flour
300 ml/½ pint dry
   white wine

150 ml/¼ pint chicken
   stock
juice of 1 lemon
seasoning
1 tablespoon chopped
   parsley

1 Peel and cook the artichokes in boiling salted water until just tender, about 15-20 minutes depending on size.
2 Melt the butter in a pan. Add the mushrooms and cook, stirring for a few minutes.
3 Stir in the flour, then gradually add the wine, stock and lemon juice. Season, bring to the boil and cook for a few minutes.
4 Drain the artichokes, add to the mushrooms and cook for a few minutes; then stir in the parsley and serve immediately.

Creamed broad beans and marrow

You will need for 6 servings:

METRIC/IMPERIAL

1 kg/2 lb fresh young
   broad beans
1 small marrow
50 g/2 oz unsalted
   butter
2 tablespoons
   chopped fresh
   tarragon or 1
   tablespoon dried

2 tablespoons water
seasoning
6 tablespoons double
   cream

1 Shell the broad beans.
2 Peel the marrow, cut into 2-cm/1-inch slices, halve these and remove the seeds with a spoon.
3 Cut the marrow into 1-cm/½-inch wide lengths.
4 Bring a pan of salted water to the boil, add the broad beans and cook fairly briskly for 10 minutes.
5 Meanwhile, place the butter, tarragon, water and seasoning in another saucepan with the marrow, cover and cook briskly for 10 minutes, until the marrow is just tender.
6 Drain the beans and keep on one side.

7 Strain the marrow into a colander, reserving the liquor.

8 Return liquor to the pan and reduce quickly to 2 tablespoons.

9 Stir in the cream and heat until cream bubbles and reduces a little.

10 Add the broad beans and marrow to the sauce, heat through and serve at once.

Sprouts with celery and cream

You will need for 3-4 servings:
METRIC/IMPERIAL
450 g/1 lb Brussels sprouts	150 ml/¼ pint single cream
3 sticks celery	salt and freshly ground black pepper
600 ml/1 pint chicken stock	
15 g/½ oz butter	

1 Trim the sprouts and cut a cross in the base of each.

2 Trim and wash the celery, cut into slices.

3 Bring the stock to the boil, add the vegetables and cook for about 8 minutes until just tender.

4 Drain the vegetables well (reserving the stock for a soup).

5 Melt the butter in a saucepan and add the cream and seasonings.

6 Return the vegetables to the pan and toss.

7 Serve at once.

Variations:

1 Lightly brown a few flaked almonds in the butter before adding the cream.

2 Stir in chopped chives or fresh thyme at the last minute.

Gingered sprouts

You will need for 4 servings:
METRIC/IMPERIAL
450 g/1 lb sprouts	4 tablespoons ginger wine
50 g/2 oz butter	2 pieces preserved ginger
50 g/2 oz blanched almonds	seasoning
grated rind of 1 lemon	
2 tablespoons lemon juice	

1 Wash and trim the sprouts. Cook in boiling salted water for 3-4 minutes, then drain.

2 Melt the butter in a pan, add the almonds and cook gently, stirring occasionally, until a light golden brown.

3 Add the lemon rind, juice, ginger wine and sprouts.

4 Cook for a few minutes until the sprouts are tender.

5 Cut up the ginger and add to the sprouts; season to taste and serve immediately.

Variation:

Omit the lemon rind and juice. Substitute dry sherry instead of the ginger wine and pieces of ginger.

Sweet and sour cabbage

You will need for 4-6 servings:
METRIC/IMPERIAL
1 kg/2 lb red cabbage	1 tablespoon red wine vinegar
1 large onion	seasoning
50 g/2 oz butter or margarine	150 ml/¼ pint chicken or vegetable stock
350 g/12 oz cooking apples	25 g/1 oz sultanas

1 Cut the cabbage in quarters, remove the hard core and shred the cabbage finely.

2 Prepare and chop onion.

3 Melt the butter or margarine in a flameproof dish.

4 Add the cabbage and onion, toss in the butter or margarine and cook gently for 10 minutes, stirring frequently.

5 Peel the apples and grate coarsely.

6 Add the remaining ingredients and mix together well.

7 Cover and cook in a moderate oven (160°C, 325°F, Gas Mark 3) for about 1 hour.

Sugar-glazed carrots

You will need for 6 servings:
METRIC/IMPERIAL
1 kg/2 lb small carrots	4 tablespoons stock or water
50 g/2 oz butter	1 tablespoon chopped parsley
3 teaspoons sugar	
seasoning	

1 Scrape the carrots and cut into equal sizes if necessary.

2 Melt the butter in a saucepan and add the sugar, seasoning and stock. Add the carrots.

3 Cover and cook very gently, shaking the pan occasionally, for 20-30 minutes depending on size, until just tender.

4 Serve at once, sprinkled with chopped parsley.

Celeriac fritters

You will need for 4-6 servings:
METRIC/IMPERIAL
2 medium-sized celeriac roots	pinch salt
salt	1 small egg, lightly beaten
little lemon juice	150 ml/¼ pint milk
for the batter:	1 tablespoon oil
100 g/4 oz plain flour	1 egg white

1 Peel the celeriac and wash well.

2 Cut into quarters and then into long strips about 1 cm/½ inch wide.

3 Place in a pan of boiling salted water with a little lemon juice and poach for 10 minutes until partly cooked. Drain well.

4 Meanwhile, make the batter. Sieve the flour and salt and make a well in the centre.

5 Add the beaten egg and the milk and whisk well, gradually incorporating the flour to make a smooth batter.
6 Beat well, then add the oil.
7 Whisk the egg white until stiff and fold gently into the batter.
8 Dip the pieces of celeriac into the batter and deep fry them a few at a time in hot fat until crisp and golden.
9 Drain on absorbent paper and serve hot, with tar-tare sauce or a good tomato relish.

Buttered courgettes

You will need for 6 servings:

METRIC/IMPERIAL

750 g/1½ lb courgettes	1 tablespoon oil
salt	1 tablespoon lemon
40 g/1½ oz butter	juice

1 Wash and wipe the courgettes on kitchen paper.
2 Trim off the ends and cut into fairly thin slices. Place in a colander, sprinkling each layer with a little salt.
3 Cover and leave to drain for about an hour.
4 Pat dry on kitchen paper.
5 Heat the butter and oil in a large frying pan. Add the courgettes and stir to coat in the fat.
6 Cover and cook over a very low heat for about 10 minutes, shaking the pan occasionally so the courgettes cook evenly.
7 Sprinkle with lemon and serve with the juices.

Parsnip-stuffed courgettes

You will need for 6 servings:

METRIC/IMPERIAL

6 medium-sized courgettes	25 g/1 oz butter
	pepper
salt	¼ teaspoon nutmeg
450 g/1 lb parsnips	

1 Wipe the courgettes, trim each end and place in boiling salted water. Simmer for 6 minutes, depending on size, until just tender.
2 Remove from the water with tongs or a slotted spoon and place in a colander under cold running water for one minute.
3 Peel and cut the parsnips, place in the boiling water and simmer for 15 minutes until soft.
4 Cut the courgettes in half lengthways and place in a greased baking dish.
5 Using the tip of a teaspoon, remove all the soft centre of each courgette and place in a bowl or blender.
6 Add to this the cooked and drained parsnips and the butter, nutmeg and pepper. Mash until fairly smooth.

7 Pile the mixture into empty courgette halves and bake in a preheated moderately hot oven (190°C, 375°F, Gas Mark 5) for 10 minutes.
Variation:
Sprinkle with a little grated cheese.

Braised fennel

You will need for 4-5 servings:

METRIC/IMPERIAL

1 kg/2 lb fennel root	juice of 1 lemon
50 g/2 oz lean streaky bacon	seasoning
	chopped parsley
25 g/1 oz butter or margarine	

1 Remove any discoloured parts from the fennel and trim the tops.
2 Cut the root into thin slices and place in an oven-proof dish.
3 Remove rind from the bacon and cut into 1-cm/½-inch strips.
4 Dot the fennel with the bacon and butter.
5 Pour the lemon juice over the fennel with the seasoning.
6 Cover and cook in a moderate oven (180°C, 350°F, Gas Mark 4) for 1¼ hours, turning the fennel once during cooking.
7 When tender, strain off the juices, place a pan and reduce by about half.
8 Pour over the fennel and sprinkle with chopped parsley.

Parsnip fritters

You will need for 4 servings:

METRIC/IMPERIAL

450 g/1 lb parsnips	75 ml/2½ fl oz tepid
50 g/2 oz plain flour	water
salt	1 egg white
2 teaspoons corn oil	corn oil for frying

1 Peel the parsnips and cut into quarters. Cook in boiling salted water for about 15-20 minutes until just tender. The time will depend on the age of the parsnips.
2 To make the batter, sieve the flour into a small bowl with the salt.
3 Gradually blend in the oil and water, removing all lumps.
4 Allow the batter to stand while the parsnips are cooking.
5 Drain the parsnips and dry on kitchen paper.
6 Whisk the egg white until stiff and dry and fold into the batter mixture until the egg white has been well mixed in.
7 Fill a saucepan with oil to a depth of 5 cm/2 inches and heat until a piece of bread turns a golden colour in 30 seconds when put into the oil.

8 Dip some of the parsnips in the batter, remove excess and fry gently in the oil for about 4 minutes, until the fritters are a golden colour.

9 Remove and drain on kitchen paper. Keep hot.

10 Batter and fry remaining parsnips and serve at once.

Peas and ham

You will need for 6 servings:
METRIC/IMPERIAL

450 g/1 lb fresh shelled peas	2 teaspoons plain flour
50 g/2 oz butter or margarine	100 g/4 oz cooked ham, cut into strips
100 ml/4 fl oz water	150 ml/¼ pint double cream
1 teaspoon sugar seasoning	

1 Wash the peas and drain.

2 Place the butter or margarine, water, sugar and seasoning into a pan, bring to the boil.

3 Add the peas, cover pan and simmer for 15-20 minutes or until just tender.

4 Blend the flour with a little cold water, add some of the hot liquid.

5 Stir into the peas, bring to the boil, stirring and simmer for 2 minutes.

6 Add the ham, stir in the cream, heat through gently but do not boil.

Variations:

1 Use chicken stock instead of water.

2 Add sliced spring onions to the peas just 5 minutes before the end of the cooking time.

3 Add small pickling onions, peeled and left whole, with the peas.

Peas and carrots in sauce

You will need for 4 servings:
METRIC/IMPERIAL

225 g/8 oz fresh podded peas	salt
225 g/8 oz small young carrots, scraped	15 g/½ oz butter
	15 g/½ oz plain flour
	pepper

1 Cook the vegetables in 150 ml/¼ pint salted water.

2 Cover and cook gently until just tender 12-15 minutes.

3 Blend the butter and flour together to make a beurre manié.

4 Add pieces of this to the cooked vegetables, stirring gently to break up and thicken the liquid the vegetables were cooked in.

5 Bring to the boil and cook for 2 minutes.

6 Taste and adjust seasonings.

Jacket potatoes

You will need for 4 servings:
METRIC/IMPERIAL

4 large potatoes	50 g/2 oz cheese, grated
corn oil	
1 teaspoon Marmite	
50 g/2 oz butter, softened	

1 Wash the potatoes and prick with a fork. Rub all over with a little oil.

2 Place on the centre shelf of a preheated moderately hot oven (200°C, 400°F, Gas Mark 6) and cook for 1 hour.

3 Meanwhile, blend the Marmite and butter together.

4 When the potatoes are cooked, cut a cross in the centre of each and pinch open.

5 Top each with grated cheese and a spoonful of the Marmite and butter mixture.

Variations:

1 Peel and cut a large onion into slices, separate into rings and fry in butter or oil until browned. Divide among the potatoes.

2 Fry chopped onion and cut up bacon pieces until crisp and serve in each potato.

3 When cooked, cut the potatoes in half lengthwise. Scoop out the potato and mash with a little butter, grated cheese and pickle. Return to the potato halves.

4 When cooked, cut potatoes in half lengthwise, make a slight hollow and break a small egg into each. Dot with a little butter, return to the oven and bake for 4-5 minutes, until the egg is just set.

5 Top each potato with a little crumbled blue cheese and crispy bacon.

6 Sprinkle grated cheese and a little grated onion into halved potatoes and placed under the grill to melt the cheese.

7 Spoon a mixture of soured cream and chives into each potato just before serving. This is especially good for serving with steak.

Potato croquettes

You will need for 8 croquettes:
METRIC/IMPERIAL

450 g/1 lb old potatoes	1 egg, beaten with 2 teaspoons cold water
15 g/½ oz butter	
2 egg yolks	50 g/2 oz fresh breadcrumbs
seasoning	
to coat:	
flour	

1 Peel the potatoes and cut into even-sized pieces. Put into a pan, cover with cold salted water and cook until just tender.

2 Strain and put potatoes in the uncovered pan over heat to dry out.

3 Mash or sieve potatoes until smooth.

4 Beat in the butter, egg yolks and seasoning.

5 Sprinkle flour lightly on a board and flour the hands.

6 Shape 8 equal portions of the potato into cylinders.

7 Dip in the beaten egg and coat finely with bread-crumbs.

8 Fry in deep fat heated to 185°C, 375°F until golden brown.

9 Drain on kitchen paper and serve hot.

Variations:

1 Shape croquette mixture into balls about 2.5 cm/1 inch across. Coat with beaten egg and almond nibs instead of breadcrumbs.

2 Add 50 g/2 oz grated cheese to croquette mixture.

3 Add ½ teaspoon concentrated curry sauce to croquette mixture.

Caramelised potatoes

You will need for 3-4 servings:
METRIC/IMPERIAL

750 g/1½ lb small new potatoes	25 g/1 oz unsalted butter
25 g/1 oz castor sugar	

1 Scrub the potatoes and boil gently in their skins until just tender, 15-20 minutes depending on size.

2 Drain, peel the potatoes and rinse in cold water.

3 Heat the sugar gently in a clean dry frying pan until it just melts. Add the butter.

4 Drain the potatoes well and add to the pan.

5 Heat gently until the potatoes are evenly glazed and lightly browned.

6 Serve with pork chops, cooked ham, gammon steaks, etc.

Note:

A very low heat is required for the sugar. It does melt eventually and caramelise. This, of course, is an important stage as the flavour depends on its success.

Buttered new potatoes with fennel

You will need for 4 servings:
METRIC/IMPERIAL

450 g/1 lb small new potatoes	2 tablespoons chopped fresh fennel leaves
4 tablespoons water	seasoning
50 g/2 oz butter	

1 Scrub the potatoes and put into a pan in one layer.

2 Add the water and butter. Cover and cook fairly gently for 15-20 minutes, until potatoes are tender.

3 Serve hot with juices from the pan, sprinkled with fennel leaves and seasoning.

Caraway potato fritters

You will need for 4-6 servings:
METRIC/IMPERIAL

450 g/1 lb old potatoes	seasoning
1 large onion	½ teaspoon caraway seeds
50 g/2 oz flour	butter and oil for frying
2 eggs, beaten	

1 Peel the potatoes and onion, grate coarsely and drain on absorbent paper.

2 Mix the vegetables with the flour, eggs, seasoning and caraway seeds.

3 Heat butter and oil to cover the base of a frying pan.

4 Place spoonfuls of the mixture in the pan and cook about 10 minutes, turning to brown both sides.

5 Drain and serve hot.

Potato leek cake

You will need for 4-6 servings:
METRIC/IMPERIAL

625 g/1¼ lb potatoes	seasoning
350 g/12 oz leeks	50 g/2 oz butter, melted
1½ teaspoon dried mixed herbs	

1 Cover the base of a 15-cm/6-inch cake tin with buttered paper.

2 Peel potatoes and slice them very thinly.

3 Trim and wash the leeks and slice them thinly.

4 Fill the prepared tin with alternate layers of potato and leeks, overlapping the slices and sprinkling with herbs and seasoning.

5 Finish with a layer of potato, pour the melted butter over the top and press greaseproof paper firmly on to the vegetables.

6 Bake in a moderately hot oven (190°C, 375°F, Gas Mark 5) for about 1 hour.

7 Test vegetables by piercing with a fine skewer.

8 Invert the tin on to a serving dish and serve the cake hot, cut into wedges.

Duchesse potatoes

You will need for 4 servings:
METRIC/IMPERIAL

1 kg/2 lb potatoes	25 g/1 oz butter
1 egg	3 tablespoons milk
seasoning	

1 Peel the potatoes and boil in the usual way.

2 Drain well and leave to dry off over a low heat.

3 Mash or sieve the potato to remove all lumps.

4 Break the egg into a cup and beat with a fork. Add to the potatoes, reserving a little for glazing.

5 Season the potatoes, add the butter and 2 tablespoons of the milk.

6 Beat well until light and fluffy.

7 Place in a large piping bag fitted with a fluted vegetable nozzle.
8 Pipe swirls on a well-greased baking sheet.
9 Add the remaining milk to the last bit of egg.
10 Brush carefully over the potatoes.
11 Place in a hot oven (220°C, 425°F, Gas Mark 7) for 15 minutes to brown lightly.

Variations:

1 Add a few mixed herbs and grated lemon rind to the potato.
2 Chopped parsley, finely grated cheese and even a little grated orange rind are interesting additions, depending on what the potatoes are being served with.

Creamed potato and carrot

You will need for 4 servings:

METRIC/IMPERIAL

450 g/1 lb old potatoes	65 g/2½ oz natural yoghurt
100 g/4 oz carrots	seasoning
25 g/1 oz butter	pinch grated nutmeg

1 Peel the potatoes, cut into even-sized pieces and cook in boiling salted water until tender.
2 Strain and return in the uncovered pan to the heat to dry off potatoes.
3 Mash them thoroughly.
4 Peel and grate the raw carrots.
5 Mix them with the potato, butter, yoghurt, seasoning, and nutmeg if liked.
6 Heat through and serve at once.

Potatoes boulangère

You will need for 3-4 servings:

METRIC/IMPERIAL

750 g/1½ lb potatoes	
225 g/8 oz onions	50 g/2 oz butter, melted
seasoning	*to garnish:*
good pinch grated nutmeg	chopped parsley
150 ml/¼ pint stock	

1 Peel potatoes and onions.
2 Cut potatoes in fairly small cubes and roughly chop the onions.
3 Butter a 1-litre/2-pint pie dish.
4 Mix potatoes and onions with seasoning and nutmeg in the dish.
5 Add the stock and pour melted butter over the top.
6 Cover with foil and bake in a moderately hot oven (190°C, 375°F, Gas Mark 5) for 35 minutes.
7 Take off the foil and add a little more stock if potatoes have absorbed it all. Continue cooking, uncovered, for about 15 minutes, until vegetables are tender and browned on top.
8 Serve hot, sprinkled with chopped parsley.

Baked Swiss chard

You will need for 4 servings:

METRIC/IMPERIAL

50 g/2 oz butter	175 g/6 oz sliced Swiss cheese
50 g/2 oz brown breadcrumbs	little flour
225 g/8 oz Swiss chard	seasoning

1 Using half the butter, grease an ovenproof dish approximately 20 cm/8 inches in diameter and sprinkle with half the breadcrumbs.
2 Wash and dry the chard and shred roughly.
3 Arrange alternate layers of half the chard and half the sliced cheese and a sprinkling of flour, salt and pepper.
4 Repeat with the remaining ingredients, top with remaining breadcrumbs and dot with the remaining butter.
5 Bake in a preheated moderate oven (180°C, 350°F, Gas Mark 4) for 15 minutes.

Stuffed tomatoes

You will need for 4 servings:

METRIC/IMPERIAL

8 large firm tomatoes	2 level tablespoons mayonnaise
1 (99-g/3½-oz) can tuna fish	seasoning
100 g/4 oz cooked rice	*to garnish:*
6 stuffed green olives, chopped	watercress

1 Cut the tomatoes in half horizontally, making a zig-zag edge. Scoop out the inside.
2 Drain the tuna fish and flake; add to the rice, olives and mayonnaise, mix well and season to taste.
3 Pile the mixture into the tomato cases, place on a serving dish and garnish with sprigs of watercress.

Variation:

Omit the rice and use a small (198-g/7-oz) can drained sweet corn and chopped parsley for colour.

Freezing and Salting

Freezing

Most vegetables can be preserved by freezing and can compare favourably with fresh in both nutrition and quality.

Vegetables should be young and fresh. Correctly prepared and packaged they can be kept in the freezer from one season to the next. Vegetables with a high water content lose their crispness, which cannot be restored, and become limp in thawing, e.g. tomatoes, onions, courgettes, etc.

It is necessary to blanch vegetables for long-term storage. The vegetables are prepared in the usual way as for general use and scalded for a few moments in boiling water. This inactivates the enzymes and prevents off flavours and colour change developing during the long storage. In cases of emergency, when perhaps going on holiday, rather than miss some of the crop it is possible to freeze without blanching but for very short term storage only.

Blanching

A large container is required with a wire basket. Small quantities like 450 g/1 lb of prepared vegetables should be blanched at a time, so the water returns to the boil quickly and then the vegetables are timed from this moment. See chart for each vegetable. The same water can be used for 6 or 7 consecutive batches of the same vegetable. Have a container of ice-cold water ready to plunge the vegetables into so they cool as quickly as possible for the same length of time as the blanching; then drain well.

The vegetables can either be spread on trays and frozen openly, or packed into freezer bags in suitable portion sizes for the family, or put into rigid containers.

Asparagus

To prepare: Grade by thickness of stems. Wash, scrape and trim to equal lengths to fit container. Do not tie in bundles.
Blanching time: Thin stems – 2 minutes. Thick stems – 4 minutes.

Aubergine

Best cooked and frozen in a ratatouille.

Broad beans

To prepare: Use only young beans. Pod and grade. Really young beans can be frozen in the pod. Top and tail and cut into 1 cm/½ inch lengths.
Blanching time: 3 minutes.

Beans – French and runner

To prepare: Select fresh tender beans that snap easily. Wash and trim, leave whole or cut in half for French beans or slice thickly for runner beans.
Blanching time: Whole beans – 2 minutes. Cut beans – 1 minute.

Beetroot

To prepare: Use small beetroot and cook whole until tender. Rub off skins and pack in rigid containers.

Broccoli

To prepare: Choose compact heads. Trim stalks to even lengths. Divide into thin, medium and thick stems.
Blanching time: 3-4-5 minutes depending on thickness.

Brussels sprouts

To prepare: The smaller sprouts will give better results. Trim stalks, remove discoloured leaves. Cut a cross into the stalk and wash.
Blanching time: 3 minutes.

Carrots

To prepare: Use small whole carrots. Wash and cut off tops and root. Remove skin after blanching.
Blanching time: 5 minutes.

Cauliflower

To prepare: Use firm white heads, remove outer leaves and separate into sprigs; try to keep an even size.
Blanching time: 3 minutes.

Corn on the cob

To prepare: Choose young cobs. Strip husk and silk, trim ends and wash.
Blanching time: 4-6 minutes depending on size.

Corn kernels

To prepare: As corn on the cob. Strip off kernels after blanching.

Courgettes

To prepare: Trim and wash, cut into 2-cm/1-inch slices, or use in ratatouille.
Blanching time: 2-3 minutes.

Onions

To prepare: 1. Peel and slice. 2. Chop. 3. Small – leave whole.
Blanching time: 1-2 minutes.

Peas

To prepare: Choose young tender peas, shell and sort carefully.
Blanching time: 1 minute.

Peppers – red and green

To prepare: Wash and remove seeds and core by cutting round the stem. Cut into halves or slice or leave whole for stuffing later. Can be blanched, stuffed and frozen.
Blanching time: 2 minutes.

Potato chips

To prepare: Prepare chips and blanch in cold water, dry well and fry in oil up to the first frying. See note in A-Z Vegetables on frying potatoes (page 10). Cool quickly and freeze in a single layer on a tray. Pack in bags.

Spinach

To prepare: Pick over leaves carefully and remove thick stems. Wash very thoroughly at least twice to remove grit.
Blanching time: Only small quantities at a time so the leaves do not stick together. 3 minutes.

Turnips or Swedes

To prepare: Freeze only young vegetables. Peel and cut into dice.
Blanching time: 3 minutes.

Salting

Salted beans

This recipe is suitable for runner or French beans. To prepare runner beans, wash, dry well, top and tail and slice into 5-cm/2-inch lengths. To prepare French beans, wash, dry well, top and tail and either cut in half or leave whole. Always use block kitchen salt, allowing 450 g/1 lb salt to each 1.4 kg/3 lbs prepared beans. It is important to weigh the salt accurately for if too little is used the beans will not keep and will become slimy. Ordinary table salt is not satisfactory.

Sterilise all containers and equipment with boiling water before using. Glass or earthenware jars are best to pack the beans in.

Place a layer of salt in the base of the jars, add a layer of sliced beans and press them down firmly. Cover them with another layer of salt and then a further layer of beans. Continue in this way, pressing each layer of beans down firmly until the jar is full, ending with a layer of salt.

Cover the jar and leave to stand for 48 hours, by which time the salt will have begun to dissolve, a brine will have formed and the beans will have shrunk sufficiently to allow more beans and salt to be packed into the jar.

Press the beans down firmly again, cover the jar with a cork or a thick layer of greaseproof paper and tie down securely.

If the beans are not keeping well it is either because too little salt was used or the beans were not packed down firmly, thus leaving pockets of air which will decompose the beans.

To use: take out as many beans as required, re-cover the jar securely. Rinse the beans under cold water, place in a bowl of warm water and leave to soak for 2 hours. (The longer the beans have been preserved the longer they will need soaking.) Then cook in boiling water until tender. No extra salt need be added.

Other vegetables, such as cabbage, carrots, cucumber, and peas, can also be salted.

Chutneys and Pickles

Bottling and labelling

The bottling of chutneys, pickles and relishes is important. They should be bottled while hot in sterilised clean warm jars. There is no necessity to use special jars but an airtight acid-proof cover is essential to prevent evaporation and corrosion.

Jars with corks can be used. Old corks should be boiled beforehand and a piece of greaseproof paper placed between the jar and cork.

Vinegar-proof papers are sold for this purpose. A cover of greaseproof paper over the jar and a round of cotton material dipped in melted paraffin wax over the top is good. Also some plastic covers are excellent.

Label and date jars clearly.

White apple chutney

You will need for approximately 1-1.5 kg/2-3 lb:
METRIC/IMPERIAL

1 kg/2 lb cooking apples, peeled and cored	175 g/6 oz sugar
350 g/12 oz onions, peeled	150 ml/¼ pint distilled white vinegar

1 Slice the apples and chop the onions. Place together in a saucepan with the remaining ingredients.
2 Bring to the boil, cover and simmer for 1 hour. Uncover and cook gently for a further 50-60 minutes.
3 Meanwhile, sterilise and have ready warmed jars.
4 Bottle, cover and label the chutney.
5 Serve with cold meats, poultry, cheese or grilled lamb chops.

Variations:
1 Mint chutney: add 175 g/6 oz chopped fresh mint.
2 Lemon chutney: add grated rind and juice of 3 lemons.

Pickled beetroot

You will need for approximately 2.5 kg/5 lb:
METRIC/IMPERIAL

2.5 kg/5 lb small beetroots, uncooked	1 tablespoon allspice berries
1.2 litres/2 pints malt or white vinegar	1 tablespoon mustard seed
50 g/2 oz whole pickling spice or the following spices:	1 cinnamon stick
	4 peppercorns
1 tablespoon whole cloves	1 blade mace

1 Wash the beetroots well and place in a large saucepan of cold salted water. Bring to the boil, cover and cook for 1½-2 hours, depending on the size.
2 Drain, leave to get cold then rub off the skins and trim off the top and base.
3 Slice the beetroots thinly.
4 Meanwhile, to make the spiced vinegar, place the vinegar and pickling spice or combined spices in a bowl and stand in a saucepan of water.
5 Cover the bowl with a plate and bring the water in the pan slowly to the boil.
6 Remove from the heat and leave the bowl standing in the hot water for 2 hours.
7 Strain the vinegar to remove the spices.
8 Have ready sterilised jars with lids.
9 Pack the sliced beets into the jars, not too tightly.
10 Add a little salt if liked and pour over the spiced vinegar to cover them.
11 Seal tightly, and label.

Beetroot relish

You will need for approximately 2.5 kg/5 lb:
METRIC/IMPERIAL

450 g/1 lb cooking apples	600 ml/1 pint malt vinegar
450 g/1 lb onions	450 g/1 lb granulated sugar
2 tablespoons horseradish sauce	1 kg/2 lb cooked beetroot
2 teaspoons salt	
pepper	
¼ teaspoon ground cloves	

1 Peel the apples and onions; core the apples.
2 Mince both and put into a pan with the horseradish, salt, pepper, cloves, vinegar and sugar.
3 Heat gently and stir occasionally until the sugar dissolves.
4 Simmer for 20 minutes.

5 Meanwhile, peel and mince the beetroot.

6 Add to the pan and continue simmering for 15-20 minutes.

7 Put hot relish into warmed jars.

8 Cover with acid-resistant tops when cold.

Pickled red cabbage

You will need for approximately 1 kg/2-2½ lb:

METRIC/IMPERIAL

1 kg/2-2½ lb medium red cabbage	2 teaspoons whole black peppercorns
cooking salt	blade mace
750 ml/1¼ pints white vinegar	1 teaspoon whole cloves
2 teaspoons allspice berries	

1 Remove any damaged outer leaves of the cabbage, halve and remove the centre core.

2 Shred fairly finely and layer in a bowl with salt sprinkled liberally between each layer, finishing with a layer of salt.

3 Cover the bowl and leave to stand for 24 hours.

4 Place the vinegar and spices in a pan, bring to the boil and boil for 1 minute; then remove from the heat and leave to get cold.

5 Strain off the spices and store the vinegar in a sealed bottle until the next day.

6 Drain the cabbage and rinse to remove excess salt.

7 Dry thoroughly and pack into sterilised jars.

8 Pour the cold spiced vinegar over the cabbage to within 2 cm/¾ inch of the top.

9 Seal tightly and use within 3 months or the cabbage will start to lose its crispness.

Carrot and orange chutney

You will need for approximately 1-1.5 kg/2-3 lb:

METRIC/IMPERIAL

350 g/12 oz carrots, peeled and trimmed	175 g/6 oz soft brown sugar
225 g/8 oz onions, peeled	50 g/2 oz raisins
225 g/8 oz cooking apples, peeled and cored	2 cloves
	4 oranges, grated rind and juice
	450 ml/¾ pint vinegar

1 Grate the carrots and chop the onions. Grate the cooking apples.

2 Place the prepared ingredients together in a large saucepan with the sugar, raisins, cloves and grated rind and juice of the oranges. Pour on the vinegar.

3 Bring to the boil, cover and simmer for 40 minutes. Remove the lid and simmer for a further 40 minutes, until fairly thick.

4 Meanwhile, sterilise and have ready warmed jars. Pot the chutney, leave for a few minutes, then cover tightly and label.

5 Serve with cold meats, poultry or cheese.

Pickled ridge cucumbers

You will need for 450 g/1 lb:

METRIC/IMPERIAL

450 g/1 lb small or medium-sized ridge cucumbers	6 peppercorns
	4 cloves
salt	15 g/½ oz sugar
450 ml/¾ pint cider vinegar	1 small onion, thinly sliced

1 Trim the stalks off the cucumbers. Wash and drain, then place in a bowl and cover liberally with salt. Leave for approximately 2 hours, then rinse and drain thoroughly.

2 Place the vinegar in a saucepan together with the peppercorns, cloves and sugar. Bring to the boil then simmer for 3-4 minutes. Strain and bring back to the boil.

3 Place the cucumbers in warmed jars together with the chopped onion and pour over the boiling vinegar. Cover tightly.

Cucumber relish

You will need for 1 kg/2 lb:

METRIC/IMPERIAL

1 kg/2 lb medium-sized ridge cucumbers	1 teaspoon ground ginger
	900 ml/1½ pints distilled white vinegar
450 g/1 lb onions	
8 cloves	225 g/8 oz sugar
pinch turmeric	

1 Trim, wash and dry the cucumbers, then grate coarsely. Place in a basin and sprinkle liberally with salt. Leave for 2-3 hours; then rinse and drain thoroughly on kitchen paper.

2 Peel and chop the onions. Place in a saucepan together with the cucumber and remaining ingredients. Bring to the boil, cover and simmer for 30-40 minutes.

3 Have ready warmed clean jars, bottle the relish and cover immediately.

4 Serve with cold meats, cheese and fish.

Marrow chutney

You will need for approximately 3 kg/6 lb:

METRIC/IMPERIAL

1.5 kg/3 lb marrow	75 g/3 oz pickling spice
450 g/1 lb onions	
450 g/1 lb cooking apples	1 kg/2 lb demerara sugar
225 g/8 oz chopped dates	1 teaspoon salt
225 g/8 oz sultanas	600 ml/1 pint vinegar
50 g/2 oz ground ginger	

1 Peel and dice the marrow; place in a large pan.
2 Peel and chop the onions and apples and place in the pan with the dates, sultanas and ginger.
3 Place the pickling spice in muslin and tie up carefully; place in the pan with the remaining ingredients.
4 Cover and heat gently, stirring to dissolve the sugar; then simmer gently for 1½ hours. Remove the muslin bag.
5 Allow to cool before bottling in clean jars, seal and label.

Sweet and sour onions

You will need for approximately 1 kg/2 lb:

METRIC/IMPERIAL

1 kg/2 lb pickling onions	600 ml/1 pint malt vinegar
225 g/8 oz salt	15 g/½ oz pickling spice
2.25 litres/4 pints water	
225 g/8 oz demerara sugar	

1 Place the onions in a large saucepan with the salt and water and stir.
2 Put a plate on top to keep the onions under the brine.
3 Leave for 12 hours.
4 Peel the onions carefully and return to the brine for a further 24-36 hours.
5 Meanwhile, to make up the spiced vinegar, dissolve the sugar in the vinegar over a low heat, stir in the spice, bring slowly to the boil and boil for a few seconds.
6 Leave with the spices to become cold.
7 Drain the onions well and pack into jars suitable for vinegar and pickles.
8 Strain the vinegar and pour over the onions. Cover and seal. Leave for 3-4 months before eating.

Red pepper and courgette pickle

You will need for approximately 1-1.5 kg/2-3 lb:

METRIC/IMPERIAL

300 g/10 oz red peppers	50 g/2 oz raisins
300 g/10 oz courgettes	50 g/2 oz sultanas
salt	225 g/8 oz brown sugar
300 g/10 oz cooking apples, peeled and cored	1 teaspoon ground ginger
350 g/12 oz onions, peeled	½ teaspoon turmeric
	300 ml/½ pint vinegar

1 Remove the seeds and stalk from the peppers and chop roughly, then place in a bowl.

2 Trim and roughly chop the courgettes and add to the peppers.
3 Sprinkle liberally with salt and leave to stand for several hours or overnight.
4 Drain, rinse and dry thoroughly.
5 Chop the apples and onions, then place in a saucepan.
6 Add the peppers, courgettes and remaining ingredients.
7 Bring to the boil, cover and simmer for 15 minutes. Uncover and cook for a further 60 minutes.
8 Meanwhile, sterilise and have ready warmed jars. Bottle and tightly cover the pickle. Label clearly.
9 Serve with cold or hot meats, poultry or cheese.

Green tomato chutney

You will need for approximately 1.5 kg/3 lb:

METRIC/IMPERIAL

1.5 kg/3 lb green tomatoes	1 teaspoon salt
2 medium-sized red peppers	1 medium-sized ginger root, peeled and finely chopped
350 g/12 oz onions	pinch cayenne
350 g/12 oz apples	450 g/1 lb soft brown sugar
350 g/12 oz sultanas	600 ml/1 pint malt vinegar
50 g/2 oz mustard seed	

1 Wash and slice the tomatoes, place in a large pan.
2 Wash and remove the seeds from the peppers; chop the flesh.
3 Peel and chop the onions and apples; add to the pan with the remaining ingredients.
4 Simmer very slowly for 2-3 hours until the mixture is thick but still a little runny, stirring occasionally.
5 Pour into clean warm jars, seal and label.

Red tomato chutney

You will need for approximately 2 kg/4 lb:

METRIC/IMPERIAL

2 kg/4 lb ripe tomatoes	2 teaspoons ground allspice
450 g/1 lb dessert apples	1 tablespoon salt
450 g/1 lb onions	1 tablespoon cayenne pepper
350 g/12 oz sultanas	750 g/1½ lb soft brown sugar
350 g/12 oz raisins	900 ml/1½ pints vinegar
1 teaspoon mustard powder	

1 Peel and chop the tomatoes. Peel, core and chop the apples and finely chop or mince the onions.
2 Place all the ingredients into a large pan and bring to the boil, stirring.
3 Cook gently, uncovered, for 1 hour, stirring occasionally until the ingredients are quite tender and the chutney is thick.
4 Ladle the hot chutney into warmed jars, cover, and label.

Tango tomato relish

You will need for approximately 1 kg/2 lb:

METRIC/IMPERIAL
1.5 kg/3 lb tomatoes
450 g/1 lb onions
225 g/8 oz granulated
  sugar

300 ml/½ pint malt
  vinegar
1 teaspoon salt

1 Skin and chop the tomatoes coarsely and place in a saucepan.
2 Peel and chop the onions and add to the pan with the remaining ingredients.
3 Heat gently to dissolve the sugar then simmer until the mixture becomes thick, about 1-1¼ hours.
4 Put in warm clean jars, seal and label.

Oriental pickle

You will need for approximately 1-1.5 kg/2-3 lb:

METRIC/IMPERIAL
40 g/1½ oz piece fresh
  ginger root
300 g/10 oz tomatoes
300 g/10 oz apples,
  peeled and cored
225 g/8 oz onions,
  peeled
1 large green pepper,
  core and seeds
  removed

1 large carrot, peeled
100 g/4 oz block
  cooking dates
225 g/8 oz soft light
  brown sugar
grated rind and juice
  of 1 lemon
grated rind and juice
  of 1 orange
150 ml/¼ pint vinegar

1 Cover the ginger with water, bring to the boil and simmer for 10 minutes. Drain, rinse in cold water and peel. Slice thinly.
2 Slice the tomatoes, apples, onions, green pepper and carrot.
3 Chop the dates. Place all the ingredients in a saucepan.
4 Bring to the boil, cover and simmer for 1 hour then uncover and simmer for a further 40 minutes.
5 Meanwhile, sterilise and have ready warmed jars.
6 Bottle, cover and label the pickle.
7 Serve with meats (hot or cold), poultry or cheese.

Piccalilli

You will need for approximately 2.5 kg/5 lb:

METRIC/IMPERIAL
750 g/1½ lb cucumbers
1 large cauliflower,
  weighing about
  750 g/1½ lb
  without outer
  leaves and stalk
450 g/1 lb onions
2 tablespoons salt
600 ml/1 pint white
  wine vinegar
1 tablespoon mustard
  seed
1 teaspoon black
  peppercorns

1 teaspoon allspice
  berries
1 teaspoon cloves
4 dried red chillies
100 g/4 oz demerara
  sugar
1 tablespoon flour
2 tablespoons
  turmeric
2 tablespoons dry
  mustard

1 Dice vegetables, layer in a bowl with the salt and leave for 12 hours.
2 Drain off all liquid.
3 Boil 450 ml/¾ pint of the vinegar with the mustard seed, peppercorns, allspice, cloves and chillies for 4-5 minutes.
4 Strain, discarding the spices.
5 Mix sugar, flour, turmeric and mustard with remaining vinegar in a large saucepan. Stir in the strained spiced vinegar and bring to the boil.
6 Add the vegetables to the pan. Stir to mix well and simmer, uncovered, for 10 minutes.
7 Cool for 2-3 minutes, then ladle into warm jars and cover immediately.

Rhubarb ketchup

You will need for approximately 750 ml/1¼ pints:

METRIC/IMPERIAL
350 g/12 oz rhubarb,
  trimmed and
  washed
225 g/8 oz onions,
  chopped
175 g/6 oz cooking
  apples, peeled and
  cored

175 g/6 oz granulated
  sugar
2 cloves garlic,
  crushed
½ teaspoon ground
  ginger
1 clove
300 ml/½ pint distilled
  white vinegar

1 Cut the rhubarb and place in a saucepan together with the chopped onions. Chop the apples and add with the remaining ingredients.
2 Bring to the boil, cover and simmer for 40-50 minutes.
3 Meanwhile, sterilise and have ready warmed jars or bottles.
4 Sieve or liquidise the ketchup and bottle immediately then cover tightly and label.
5 Serve with meats and poultry (cold or hot) or use in sauces and dressings.

Tomato ketchup

You will need for 750 ml/1¼ pints:

METRIC/IMPERIAL
3 kg/6 lb ripe
  tomatoes
225 g/8 oz granulated
  sugar
300 ml/½ pint malt
  vinegar
pinch cayenne pepper
1 tablespoon salt

¼ teaspoon ground
  cinnamon
¼ teaspoon ground
  ginger
¼ teaspoon ground
  cloves
¼ teaspoon ground
  mace

1 Wash and quarter tomatoes and place in a preserving pan or large saucepan.
2 Cook slowly until soft, then boil rapidly to reduce them to a pulp.
3 Press the pulp through a sieve, return to the pan and stir in the sugar, vinegar, pepper, salt and spices.

4 Heat slowly over low heat to allow the sugar to dissolve completely; then bring to the boil and boil rapidly for about 5 minutes until it is quite a thick sauce.
5 Pour into sterilised dry bottles leaving 4 cm/1½ inches unfilled at the top.
6 Scald the tops and screw on tightly.
7 To process, place on a trivet in a large saucepan and fill the pan with water to within 2.5 cm/1 inch of the tops of the bottles.
8 Heat the water to 80°C, 170°F, and simmer very gently for 20 minutes.
9 Remove the bottles and leave to cool before storing.
Note:
Non-returnable tonic bottles with screw tops are ideal. This recipe fills 3 small tonic bottles.

Salads: Introduction

There should always be a place in our diet for salads as they are delicious, healthy, nutritious and good for our figures, too. Over the last few years, people have become much more health conscious and realise the wisdom of eating salads more often both in the summer and the winter.

Salads are the ideal accompaniment to a wide range of dishes, both hot and cold, and many are hearty enough to form the basis of a main meal. I have used raw vegetables, lightly cooked vegetables and pasta as well as fruit and nuts to give varied and interesting flavours and textures.

A-Z Salad Vegetables

Basic preparation, cooking and serving

Artichokes - Jerusalem

To prepare: See Vegetables (page 6).
To cook: Boil, drain. Cool and slice.
To serve: With salad dressing or various flavoured mayonnaise.

Asparagus

To prepare: See Vegetables (page 6).
To cook: Boil or steam. Drain carefully, cool on kitchen paper.
To serve: Served with melted butter or Hollandaise sauce. Whole stems or chopped and mixed with flavoured mayonnaise in a salad.

Aubergines

To prepare: See Vegetables (page 7).
To cook: Sauté or grill.
To serve: Tossed in salad dressing.

Avocado pears

To prepare: Halve and remove stone. Leave in skin or score several times and peel off skin. Sprinkle with lemon juice to prevent discolouration.
To serve: Halves in skin (1 half per person), with vinaigrette or with filling such as shellfish. Peeled and puréed to make dressing or "dip". Peeled and sliced just before serving; tossed in dressing or mayonnaise.

Beans - broad

To prepare: See Vegetables (page 7). In pods when young, or shelled.
To cook: Boil or steam. Drain on kitchen paper.
To serve: Tossed in flavoured dressing or light mayonnaise.

Beans - French

To prepare: See Vegetables (page 7). Use whole or sliced.
To cook: Boil or steam. Rinse in cold water. Drain on kitchen paper.
To serve: Tossed in flavoured dressing.

Beans - runner

To prepare: See Vegetables (page 7). Use small whole or sliced.
To cook: Boil or steam. Rinse in cold water. Drain on kitchen paper.
To serve: Tossed in flavoured dressing or light mayonnaise.

Beetroot

To prepare: See Vegetables (page 7). Use raw, peeled and grated or sliced, or cooked, peeled sliced, cubed or grated.
To cook: Boil or steam whole. Peel when cold.
To serve: Raw or cooked in dressings or mayonnaise.

Broccoli

To prepare: See Vegetables (page 7), trim stalks quite short.
To cook: Blanch in boiling salted water, 3-4 minutes. Drain, rinse in cold water. Cool on kitchen paper.
To serve: With dressings or mayonnaise.

Brussels sprouts

To prepare: See Vegetables (page 7). Use whole small sprouts. May be shredded raw.
To cook: Blanch in boiling salted water, 2-3 minutes. Drain, rinse in cold water. Cool on kitchen paper. May be halved.
To serve: Cooked or raw in dressing or mayonnaise. Allow raw sprouts 30 minutes to marinate in dressings for flavours to blend.

Cabbage - white

To prepare: Quarter cabbage, remove core, wash in cold water. Drain. Slice finely, raw.
To serve: Tossed in dressing or mayonnaise.

Cabbage - red

To prepare: Quarter, remove core. Wash in cold water. Drain. Slice finely, raw.
To serve: Marinate in dressing for at least 30 minutes before serving.

Cabbage - Chinese

To prepare: Cut out stalk and coarse ribs. Wash in cold water and drain. Slice, shred or break in pieces.
To serve: Plain or tossed in dressing just before serving to retain crispness.

Carrots

To prepare: Skin small carrots; use whole. Scrub clean or scrape in cold water. Peel mature carrots. Wash and drain. Grate coarsely or shred. Cut in slices or cubes.
To cook: Boil new whole carrots, in salt water 4-5 minutes. Boil mature carrots, sliced or cubed, in salt water 5-10 minutes. Drain well.
To serve: Cooked whole, sliced or cubed in dressing. Raw, grated or shredded, in dressing or mayonnaise.

Cauliflower

To prepare: Separate into florets, cut off longer stalks. Wash in cold water. Drain on kitchen paper. May be sliced thinly or shredded.
To cook: Boil florets in salted water 4-5 minutes. Drain, rinse in cold water. Drain on kitchen paper.
To serve: Raw or boiled in dressing or mayonnaise. Allow 30 minutes for flavours to blend.

Celeriac

To prepare: Use raw. Peel and wash in cold water. Drain. Grate coarsely or shred.
To serve: Tossed in dressing or mayonnaise.

Celery

To prepare: Separate stems and heart. Discard tough outer stems. Scrub clean in cold water. Drain on kitchen paper. Use leaves for garnish. Cut straight or diagonally in pieces or thin slices, or chop.
To serve: Tossed in dressing or mayonnaise.

Chard

To prepare: Leaves, remove tough ribs. Wash in cold water. Drain and dry on kitchen paper. Tear into pieces or shred. Cut stalks in even-sized lengths.
To cook: Boil or steam stalks as for Vegetables (page 8). Drain well.
To serve: Leaves plain or tossed in dressing. Stalks cut in short lengths in mayonnaise.

Chicory

To prepare: Separate leaves. Cut out core. Wash in cold water. Drain well. Use leaves whole or cut in pieces.
To serve: Tossed in dressing just before serving to retain crispness. Tips often used as garnish.

Cos lettuce

To prepare: Cut off stalk, remove any tough ribs. Wash in cold water. Drain well. Use small leaves whole, larger leaves tear in pieces or slice.
To serve: Plain in green salad, tossed in dressing just before serving.

Courgettes

To prepare: See Vegetables (page 8). Use small courgettes whole. Larger ones, cut in quarters lengthwise or sliced.
To cook: Blanch in boiling salted water 2-3 minutes. Drain, rinse in cold water. Drain on kitchen paper. Sauté slices in butter.
To serve: Tossed in dressing or mayonnaise.

Cucumber

To prepare: Wipe clean. Trim off ends. Peel lengthwise in strips, retaining some peel for extra colour; or peel completely or not at all. May be shredded, cut in slices, sticks or cubes. May be sprinkled with salt and left on kitchen paper to draw out excess moisture. Rinse and dry thoroughly. May be cut in thick slices and seeds scooped out to be filled with salad mixture; or halved lengthwise and seeds scooped out for filling.
To serve: Slices, sticks, cubes, shredded in dressing. Plain as a garnish. Stuffed halves or rings as separate dish.

Endive

To prepare: See Vegetables (page 8). Tear leaves in small pieces.
To serve: Plain in green salad. Tossed in dressings. As a garnish.

Fennel

To prepare: See Vegetables (page 8). Use raw, grated or chopped. Leave whole to cook. Use leaves as garnish or chop to flavour dressings and salads.
To cook: Boil in salted water 30-40 minutes. Drain and leave until cold. Cut into slices.
To serve: Raw or cooked, tossed in dressing or mayonnaise.

Leeks

To prepare: See Vegetables (page 9). Slice thinly or shred. Use raw or cooked.
To cook: Blanch in boiling salted water 2-3 minutes. Drain, rinse in cold water. Drain on kitchen paper.
To serve: Raw or blanched, tossed in dressing.

Lettuce - round

To prepare: Trim stem and discard limp or damaged leaves. Wash carefully in cold water to avoid bruising leaves. Drain well. Use inner leaves and heart whole. Tear larger leaves in pieces or shred.
To serve: Plain in green salad, as garnish or bed. Tossed in dressing just before serving to retain crispness.

Mange tout peas

To prepare: See Vegetables (page 9). Use small whole or slice diagonally.
To cook: Blanch in boiling salted water 3-4 minutes. Drain, rinse in cold water and drain well.
To serve: Tossed in dressings.

Marrows

To prepare: Trim both ends, cut in 1-cm/½-inch slices, peel thinly, remove seeds. Cut in pieces.
To cook: Boil with herbs in salted water for 3 minutes. Drain, rinse in cold water, drain on kitchen paper.
To serve: Tossed in dressing; allow 30 minutes for flavours to blend.

Mushrooms

To prepare: See Vegetables (page 9). Remove stalks if hard. Use raw whole baby button mushrooms or slice thinly. Marinate in dressing. Slice thicker to cook.
To cook: Sauté in oil 2-3 minutes.
To serve: Raw or cooked, tossed in dressing or mayonnaise.

Mustard and cress

To prepare: Use scissors to snip through stalks, leaving roots in punnet. Wash in cold water to remove black seeds. Drain well.
To serve: Plain in green salad, as garnish. Tossed in dressings.

Onions

To prepare: Trim both ends and remove outer skin. Slice thinly or chop. May be marinated.
To serve: As garnish, tossed in dressing.

Parsnips

To prepare: See Vegetables (page 9). Cut in thin slices if not too large or cubes.
To cook: Boil in salted water or stock 5 minutes. Drain.
To serve: Tossed in dressing.

Peas

To prepare: Shell, wash and drain.
To cook: Boil in salted water with herbs and sugar. Very young peas 2 minutes, mature up to 20 minutes until just tender. Drain. Rinse in cold water. Drain.
To serve: Tossed in dressing or left raw and tossed in a salad.

Pepper - red or green

To prepare: See Vegetables (page 10). Cut in thin slices; use raw or cooked. Grill and remove skin which may be indigestible.
To cook: Sauté slices in oil 5-10 minutes, retaining crispness.
To serve: Raw or sautéed slices tossed in dressing.

Potatoes

To prepare: Scrub clean or peel.
To cook: Boil in salted water with mint, or steam. May be peeled after cooking. Use small new potatoes whole or cut in slices or cubes. Toss in salad dressing while warm to absorb dressing.
To serve: In mayonnaise.

Radishes

To prepare: Trim root end. If to be eaten with fingers, retain 1 cm/½ inch of stalk for holding, otherwise trim off all stalk. Wash in cold water. Drain. Leave small radishes whole; cut large ones in thin slices or small cubes.
For garnish:Roses: Cut with small pointed knife from stalk end almost to root end in narrow segments. Cross cut root end. Put in iced water for 'petals' to open.
Fans: Cut ½-cm/¼-inch slices through stalk end, keeping root end intact. Open out slices carefully.
Waterlilies: Slice in segments from stalk end. Put in iced water. Drain and dry.
To serve: As garnish. Small whole, sliced or cubed, tossed in dressing.

Salsify

To prepare: See Vegetables (page 11). Leave whole.
To cook: Boil in salted water with lemon or in stock 15-20 minutes. Drain. Peel and cut into slices.
To serve: Tossed in dressing.

Seakale

To prepare: Trim stalks, wash in cold water. May be used raw, cut in thin slices. To cook, cut in 5-cm/2-inch lengths.
To cook: Boil in salted water 4-5 minutes. Drain and dry thoroughly.
To serve: Raw or cooked, tossed in dressing.

Shallots

To prepare: See Vegetables (page 11). Use small whole even-sized shallots for cooking or marinate in dressing. Slice thinly to use raw.
To cook: Boil in salted water 20-25 minutes, until tender but still crisp. Drain thoroughly.
To serve: Sliced, plain or tossed in dressing.

Spinach

To prepare: Use raw. Remove stalks and ribs. Wash thoroughly in cold water. Tear in pieces or shred.
To serve: Tossed in dressing. Plain in green salad.

Spring onions

To prepare: Trim root end and some of green leaves, retaining most of them. Remove any damaged outer leaves. Wash in cold water. Drain. Use whole or sliced.
To serve: As garnish, tossed in dressing.

Swedes

To prepare: Trim both ends. Peel thickly. Wash in cold water. Drain. Use raw, grated or shredded. To cook, cut into small cubes.
To cook: Boil in salt water 10-15 minutes until just tender. Drain well.
To serve: Boiled swede marinated in dressing. Raw, tossed in dressing or mayonnaise.

Sweetcorn

To prepare: See Vegetables (page 11). Separate kernels.
To cook: Boil in salted water 5-10 minutes until just tender. Drain.
To serve: Tossed in dressing or mayonnaise.

Tomatoes

To prepare: Wipe clean, remove stalk. May be skinned. Use small whole tomatoes, or cut in slices or segments. To stuff, cut in halves or cut a 'lid' from the smooth end. Scoop out seeds and drain upside down.
Vandyke tomatoes: Cut in halves with small pointed knife making diagonal cuts through to the middle. Separate halves.
Waterlily: Cut in segments from top of smooth end almost to stalk end.
Concasséed tomatoes: Skinned, quartered and seeds removed.
To serve: As garnish. Stuffed as a starter or main salad. Slices or segments tossed with dressing and herbs.

Turnips

To prepare: Trim both ends, peel thickly. Use raw, coarsely grated or shredded. To cook, cut small turnip in slices, larger turnip in cubes.
To cook: Boil in salted water 5-10 minutes. Drain well. Marinate in dressing.
To serve: Raw grated, or cooked, tossed in dressing or mayonnaise.

Watercress

To prepare: Break off big stalks. Remove any wilted or damaged leaves. Wash in cold water. Drain well. Break into separate sprigs or shred.
To serve: Plain in green salads or as a garnish. Tossed in dressing.

Salads

Meat and poultry salads

Ham and pea salad with pineapple

You will need for 4 servings:

METRIC/IMPERIAL

225 g/8 oz shelled young peas	1½ tablespoons corn oil
225 g/8 oz slice of ham	3 tablespoons of the pineapple juice
6 spring onions	1 tablespoons white wine vinegar
1 (226-g/8-oz) can pineapple slices	pinch each of salt, pepper, dry mustard and castor sugar
for the dressing:	
50 g/2 oz Lancashire cheese, grated	

1 Cook the peas in boiling salted water for 15-20 minutes depending on tenderness and size.
2 Drain and refresh under cold water and place in a bowl.
3 Cut the ham into thin strips about 2.5 cm/1 inch long and add.
4 Trim off most of the green from the onions, wash and slice thinly and add to the peas and ham.
5 Drain the pineapple, reserving 3 tablespoons of the juice, and cut the pineapple into small segments, add to the peas. Chill well.
6 Place all the dressing ingredients into a screw-top jar and shake well.
7 Spoon the dressing over just before serving.

Bacon pasta salad

You will need for 4 servings:

METRIC/IMPERIAL

225 g/8 oz short macaroni	4 large tomatoes
1 large onion	3 tablespoons French dressing (see page 86)
1 tablespoon oil	1 clove garlic, crushed
225 g/8 oz lean streaky bacon	2 tablespoons chopped parsley

1 Bring a large pan of salted water to the boil.
2 Add the macaroni and stir. Return to the boil and cook for 12-15 minutes until just tender, stirring occasionally.
3 Prepare and chop the onion.
4 Heat the oil in a frying pan, add the onion and cook gently.
5 Meanwhile, remove the rind from the bacon and cut into pieces, add to the onion and cook for about 10 minutes, until the bacon is beginning to become crisp.

6 Drain the cooked macaroni, rinse in warm water to remove excess starch.
7 Place in a mixing bowl.
8 Drain the onion and bacon on kitchen paper and add to the macaroni.
9 Remove the skins from the tomatoes, cut into quarters and remove seeds.
10 Add the tomatoes to the macaroni.
11 Mix the French dressing and garlic together and pour over the salad.
12 Toss lightly and turn into a salad bowl. Garnish with chopped parsley.
13 Serve with a green salad and warm rolls.
Variation:
Use wholemeal pasta with cooked onions and diced cold cooked bacon.

Chef's salad

You will need for 3-4 servings:

METRIC/IMPERIAL

½ Webbs or cos lettuce	100 g/4 oz Danish blue cheese
1 bunch radishes	
5-cm/2-inch length of cucumber	5 tablespoons French dressing (see page 86)
1 small onion	
225 g/8 oz cooked bacon	

1 Wash the lettuce and tear into pieces.
2 Trim and wash radishes and cut into slices.
3 Wash and slice cucumber; prepare and thinly slice the onion.
4 Cut the bacon into thick strips and the cheese into cubes.
5 Arrange all these ingredients in alternate layers in a glass bowl.
6 Pour the dressing over the salad just before serving.

Mushroom and bacon salad

You will need for 4 servings:

METRIC/IMPERIAL

4 (1-cm/½-inch) slices white bread	3 tablespoons French dressing (see page 86)
50 g/2 oz butter or margarine	1 canned red pimiento
3 tablespoons corn oil	1 small dill cucumber
6 rashers back bacon, unsmoked	50 g/2 oz stuffed or black olives
225 g/8 oz button mushrooms	2 tablespoons chopped parsley
3 spring onions	
1 small clove garlic (optional)	

1 Remove crusts from the bread and cut bread into large cubes.
2 Melt the butter or margarine with the oil and fry the bread cubes until crisp and golden, turning frequently.
3 Remove and drain on kitchen paper.
4 Remove the rind from the bacon and cut into large pieces. Fry until slightly crisp and browned; remove and drain on kitchen paper.
5 Wash the mushrooms, slice thinly, fry slowly in the bacon fat until cooked but still firm. Allow to cool.
6 Trim the spring onions and cut into slices, place in a salad bowl.
7 Crush the garlic and add with the French dressing.
8 Cut the canned pimiento into strips.
9 Slice or dice the cucumber, add to the bowl with the olives, parsley, bacon, mushrooms and pimiento. Chill if liked.
10 Toss in the croûtons just before serving.
11 Serve with a green salad, or on a bed of shredded Webbs lettuce or Chinese cabbage.

Variation:
Use 3 teaspoons of capers instead of the cucumber.

Spring pork salad

You will need for 4 servings:
METRIC/IMPERIAL
350 g/12 oz new potatoes	1 small green pepper
seasoning	4 spring onions
1 sprig mint or apple mint	1 red eating apple
450 g/1 lb pork fillet	juice of ½ lemon
1 tablespoon corn oil	*to garnish:*
5 tablespoons Lemon-flavoured French dressing (see page 86)	lettuce
	lemon slices

1 Scrape the new potatoes and cook in boiling salted water with the mint for about 10 minutes until just tender.
2 Meanwhile, trim the pork and cut into 1-cm/½-inch cubes.
3 Heat the oil in a frying pan, add the pork and fry, stirring occasionally, for about 10 minutes.
4 Place the dressing in a bowl with the cooked pork and stir.
5 Cut the potatoes into dice and add to the pork.
6 Wash the green pepper, remove core, seeds and white pith and slice thinly.
7 Prepare and chop the spring onions.
8 Add these to the salad and toss lightly.
9 Just before serving, core and slice the apple, toss in the lemon juice and add to the salad.
10 Arrange salad on lettuce leaves and garnish with lemon slices.

Pork salad brazilia

You will need for 4 servings:
METRIC/IMPERIAL
350 g/12 oz cooked pork	1 tablespoon lemon juice
50 g/2 oz Brazil nuts, chopped	seasoning
2 oranges	½ endive
2 sticks celery	2 tomatoes, cut into segments
2 tablespoons oil	

1 Trim the fat from the pork and cut into dice.
2 Add the nuts to the pork.
3 Using a sharp knife, cut the skin and pith off the oranges and cut the segments between the membrane. Add to the bowl.
4 Prepare and trim the celery. Cut into slices and add to the pork.
5 Mix the oil, lemon juice and seasoning together in a bowl. Pour over the pork and allow to stand for 30 minutes.
6 Wash and dry the endive. Break into pieces and add to the salad with the tomatoes.
7 Toss lightly and arrange in a salad bowl.

Variations:
1 Use different nuts and a pink grapefruit when they are in season instead of the oranges.
2 Serve sprinkled with chopped chives or parsley.
3 A little freshly chopped sage added to the dressing compliments the flavour of the pork.

Crispy pork salad

You will need for 4 servings:
METRIC/IMPERIAL
350 g/12 oz cold cooked pork	seasoning
225 g/8 oz white cabbage	1 red eating apple
1 lemon	1 tablespoon freshly chopped mint
1 (142-ml/5-fl oz) carton soured cream	*to garnish:*
	5-cm/2-inch length cucumber
	watercress

1 Trim any fat from the pork and cut the meat into large dice.
2 Wash the cabbage and remove the coarse outside leaves.
3 Shred the cabbage finely and discard the thick white stalk.
4 Add to the pork.
5 Finely grate the rind from the lemon and squeeze the juice.
6 Mix the rind and juice with the soured cream and seasoning.
7 Quarter the apple, remove the core and cut the apple into thin slices.
8 Add to the dressing and toss carefully to coat the slices to prevent discoloration.
9 Add the mint. Add the dressing to the pork and cabbage.

10 Toss lightly and arrange in a dish.
11 Slice the cucumber. Garnish the salad with the cucumber and watercress.
Variation:
Garnish with tomato instead of the cucumber.

Pork and red cabbage salad

You will need for 4 servings:

METRIC/IMPERIAL

350 g/12 oz cold sliced pork	½ teaspoon celery seed
½ small red cabbage	2 sticks celery
1 small onion	5 tablespoons French
2 carrots	dressing (see page 86)

1 Trim any fat from the pork slices and cut the meat into strips. Put in a salad bowl.
2 Remove the coarse outer leaves from the cabbage.
3 Wash the cabbage, cut out the thick white stalk and shred the cabbage finely.
4 Prepare and grate the onion and carrots coarsely.
5 Add these vegetables to the bowl with the celery seed sprinkled in.
6 Wash and trim the celery, slice and add to the pork.
7 Pour in the dressing and toss the salad.
8 Serve with a green salad and brown bread.
Variations:
1 Add a few currants to the salad.
2 Use caraway seed instead of the celery seed but soak in the dressing for a while before pouring the dressing over the salad.
3 Use orange segments instead of the carrot.
4 Add some chopped apple.

Pork and beansprout salad

You will need for 4 servings:

METRIC/IMPERIAL

2 courgettes	1 teaspoon chopped fresh rosemary seasoning
50 g/2 oz button mushrooms	
225 g/8 oz lean cooked pork	3 tablespoons mayonnaise (see page 87)
225 g/8 oz beansprouts, washed	2 tablespoons ginger wine
1 orange	*to garnish:*
1 tablespoon finely chopped onion	orange slices rosemary sprigs

1 Thinly peel and slice the courgettes.
2 Wipe the mushrooms and slice them thinly.
3 Roughly shred the cooked pork and mix with the courgettes, mushrooms and beansprouts.
4 Remove the rind and all the pith from the orange. Using a sharp knife, cut the segments from between the membranes and mix into the salad together with the onion.
5 Add the rosemary and seasoning.

6 Mix the mayonnaise with the ginger wine and pour over the salad. Toss well and garnish with slices of orange and sprigs of rosemary.
7 Serve with baked potatoes and a tomato salad.
Variation:
Use cooked chicken instead of the pork and slice 2 sticks of celery instead of the courgettes. Add 50 g/ 2 oz chopped walnuts.

Hot Mexican salad

You will need for 4-5 servings:

METRIC/IMPERIAL

1 tablespoon corn oil	100 g/4 oz Cheddar cheese, grated
450 g/1 lb minced beef	½ recipe Thousand Island dressing (see page 87)
1 medium onion, chopped	
1 (432-g/15½-oz) can red kidney beans	50 g/2 oz tortilla crisps or krackerwheat biscuits
½-1 tablespoon Tabasco sauce	*to garnish:*
for the salad:	1 avocado pear (optional)
1 Webbs lettuce heart	
4 medium tomatoes, skinned and chopped	

1 Place the corn oil in a fairly large saucepan with the minced beef and onion.
2 Cook, stirring frequently, until the mince and onion are nicely browned, about 20 minutes.
3 Drain the beans and add with the Tabasco sauce, using the ½ tablespoon if using the tortilla crisps (which add a distinctive flavour) or 1 tablespoon if using the krackerwheat biscuits.
4 Heat the beans through gently.
5 Mix the salad ingredients together in a bowl breaking the biscuits into fairly large pieces.
6 Remove the pan from the heat and stir in the salad ingredients.
7 Serve at once; garnish with slices of avocado pear, if liked.

Beef salad

You will need for 4 servings:

METRIC/IMPERIAL

5 tablespoons mayonnaise (see page 87)	350 g/12 oz cold new potatoes
2 tablespoons horseradish	1 canned red pimiento
1 tablespoon chopped parsley	1 (400-g/14-oz) can artichoke hearts
350 g/12 oz cold roast beef	*to garnish:* sprigs of parsley

1 Place the mayonnaise and horseradish in a bowl with the parsley.
2 Cut beef into dice; drain and slice the potatoes.

3 Add these to the bowl and mix lightly.

4 Cut up the pimiento and add.

5 Put the salad in a dish.

6 Drain the artichoke hearts, cut into quarters and arrange on the salad.

7 Garnish with parsley. Serve with a tossed salad.

Variation:

Serve the salad on top of cold rice mixed with sliced spring onions, sweet corn and some sliced olives.

Frankfurter salad

You will need for 4-6 servings:

METRIC/IMPERIAL

750 g/1½ lb new potatoes of an even size	450 g/1 lb frankfurter sausages
4 tablespoons French dressing (see page 86)	1 dill cucumber
	5 tablespoons mayonnaise (see page 87)
1 small onion, thinly sliced	1 teaspoon whole grain mustard
1 small clove garlic, crushed	2 tablespoons chopped parsley

1 Wash the potatoes and cook in their skins for about 10-15 minutes. Drain.

2 Peel the potatoes if liked and cut into dice. Place in a bowl.

3 Pour the French dressing over the hot potatoes, add the onion and garlic and stir carefully.

4 Slice the sausages and dill cucumber.

5 Mix the mayonnaise and mustard, stir in the sausages and dill cucumber and add to the potatoes.

6 Turn into a serving dish and sprinkle with the chopped parsley.

Variations:

1 Use ½ teaspoon caraway seeds instead of the mustard.

2 Garnish with sliced hard-boiled eggs.

Salami salad bowl

You will need for 3-4 servings:

METRIC/IMPERIAL

450 g/1 lb Danish salami in a piece	1 tablespoon vinegar
2-3 green peppers	1 teaspoon Worcestershire sauce
3-4 tomatoes	
lettuce	¼ level teaspoon salt
for the dressing:	1 teaspoon sugar
3 tablespoons corn oil	

1 Cut the salami into dice.

2 Slice the green peppers and tomatoes.

3 Line a salad bowl with lettuce. Mix the salami, peppers and tomatoes and put on top of the lettuce.

4 Put the ingredients for the dressing into a screw top jar and shake well.

5 Pour over the salad just before serving.

Variations:

1 For a heartier salad, add sliced cold potatoes or cold cooked pasta.

2 Add chopped parsley for added colour.

Sweet and sour chicken salad

You will need for 4 servings:

METRIC/IMPERIAL

1 (226-g/8-oz) can pineapple rings	350 g/12 oz cold cooked chicken, cut into dice
5 tablespoons French dressing made with cider vinegar (see page 86)	1 small green pepper
	100 g/4 oz carrots
1 teaspoon soy sauce	50 g/2 oz toasted almonds
1 (454-g/16-oz) can bean sprouts	seasoning

1 Drain the juice from the pineapple (if liked, use some of the juice in the dressing and cut down on the vinegar).

2 Mix the soy sauce into the dressing.

3 Drain the bean sprouts, place in a bowl with the dressing and add the chicken.

4 Wash the pepper, remove core, seeds and white pith and cut into thin strips. Add to the bowl.

5 Peel the carrots and cut into thin strips. Add to the bowl with the toasted almonds.

6 Cut the drained pineapple segments into sections and add to the salad with seasoning.

7 Toss well and serve with plain boiled rice.

Variations:

1 Add some chopped preserved ginger.

2 Use a small tin of bean sprouts and a tin of water chestnuts, drained and thinly sliced.

3 Serve with boiled rice which has been fried in butter with onion. Serve cold. Sprinkle with paprika.

Chicken and avocado salad

You will need for 4 servings:

METRIC/IMPERIAL

175 g/6 oz carrots	6 tablespoons French dressing (see page 86)
350 g/12 oz cooked chicken, diced	
75 g/3 oz salted peanuts, chopped	to garnish:
	bunch of watercress, washed
1 ripe avocado pear	

1 Peel the carrots, grate coarsely and place in a bowl.

2 Add the chicken and peanuts.

3 Halve the avocado, peel off the skin and remove stone.

4 Cut into slices and add to the chicken.

5 Add the dressing and toss carefully.

6 Arrange in a dish with the watercress garnishing the dish.

Variation:

Replace carrots with 3 oranges cut into segments; use cold duck instead of chicken.

Curried chicken salad

You will need for 4 servings:
METRIC/IMPERIAL

175 g/6 oz long-grain rice
seasoning
1 teaspoon castor sugar
1 teaspoon curry paste
1 egg yolk
150 ml/¼ pint corn oil
2 teaspoons cider vinegar
1 small green pepper

1 (227-g/8-oz) can pineapple slices
350 g/12 oz cooked chicken, cut into dice
50 g/2 oz seedless raisins
25 g/1 oz salted peanuts
1 canned red pimiento, sliced

1 Cook rice in boiling salted water for 12-15 minutes until tender. Drain well and refresh under cold water. Place in a bowl.
2 Place the seasoning and sugar in a bowl with the curry paste and blend in the egg yolk.
3 Gradually add the corn oil drop by drop until half has been added, then add some of the cider vinegar.
4 Continue until the oil and cider vinegar are used up which should give a thick mayonnaise.
5 Wash the pepper, remove the seeds and chop the flesh.
6 Add pepper to the mayonnaise.
7 Drain the pineapple well on kitchen paper; cut the pineapple into segments.
8 Add the pineapple and chicken to the mayonnaise.
9 Add the raisins to the rice with the nuts and red pimiento.
10 Arrange the rice mixture round the edges of a serving dish and pile the chicken mixture in the centre.
11 Serve with a tomato salad, sliced banana and mango chutney.

Crunchy chicken salad

You will need for 4 servings:
METRIC/IMPERIAL

1 onion
225 g/8 oz boneless, raw chicken breast
4 tablespoons olive or corn oil
50 g/2 oz blanched almonds
1 clove garlic, crushed
350 g/12 oz Chinese cabbage leaves, washed

1 red pepper
2 tablespoons wine vinegar
juice of 1 orange
seasoning
1 ripe avocado pear
1 (227-g/8-oz) can water chestnuts
2 oranges
to garnish:
mustard and cress

1 Peel and thinly slice the onion. Cut the chicken in thin strips.
2 Heat the oil in a pan then add the almonds, garlic, onion and chicken. Cook, stirring continuously, until the chicken is cooked. Remove from the heat and leave to cool.

3 Shred the Chinese cabbage leaves; seed and slice the pepper.
4 Mix these with the cooked chicken mixture, vinegar and orange juice in a bowl. Season well.
5 Peel and slice the avocado, then mix into the salad.
6 Slice the drained water chestnuts and toss into the salad.
7 Using a sharp knife, cut the rind and pith from the oranges and cut out the segments from between the membranes. Toss into the salad.
8 Garnish with small bunches of mustard and cress and serve with granary bread or warmed French bread.

Fish salads

Spanish salad

You will need for 4 servings:
METRIC/IMPERIAL

½ cos lettuce
4 tomatoes
1 (56-g/2-oz) can anchovy fillets, drained and cut in half
100 g/4 oz peeled prawns

8 stuffed green olives, halved
8 tablespoons Lemon-flavoured French dressing (see page 86)
to garnish:
2 hard-boiled eggs

1 Wash the lettuce, drain well and tear into small pieces. Place in a salad bowl.
2 Peel and quarter the tomatoes and remove the seeds. Add to the lettuce with the anchovies, prawns and olives.
3 Make up the dressing.
4 Pour over the salad and toss lightly.
5 Decorate the bowl with the sliced hard-boiled eggs and serve at once.

Variation:
Omit the anchovies from the salad and use as a decoration.

Note:
Always chill salad just before serving and toss when required.

Spanish open sandwich

You will need for 2 servings:
METRIC/IMPERIAL

2 tablespoons thick mayonnaise (see page 87)
2 spring onions, sliced thinly
1 tablespoon chopped dill cucumber
1 hard-boiled egg, chopped
8 stuffed green olives, halved

50 g/2 oz peeled prawns
seasoning
2 slices granary bread, buttered
4 large lettuce leaves
1 slice lemon
to garnish:
parsley
prawns in shells (optional)

1 Mix together the mayonnaise, onions, cucumber, egg, olives and peeled prawns. Season to taste.
2 Put the bread on plates and cover with lettuce, letting it overlap the edges of the bread.
3 Pile the mixture into the centre of the lettuce.
4 Cut the lemon slice into two, cut through the centre flesh up to the skin and make into a twist. Put on top of the mixture.
5 Decorate dish with parsley and prawns in shells.
6 Serve as a starter or a light luncheon dish.

Prawn and olive salad

You will need for 4 servings:
METRIC/IMPERIAL
½ small red pepper
½ small green pepper
3 tablespoons Lemon-flavoured French dressing (see page 86)
225 g/8 oz peeled prawns
50 g/2 oz peanuts, chopped
½ lettuce, washed

to garnish:
1 medium-sized orange, peeled and sliced
8 stuffed green olives, halved

1 Cut the red and green peppers into thin strips about 2.5 cm/1 inch long.
2 Add the peppers to the dressing with the prawns and peanuts.
3 Toss together.
4 Arrange the lettuce in the serving dish, pile the prawn mixture on top and garnish with slices of orange.
5 Arrange the sliced olives over the top and serve.

Cauliflower, cucumber and shrimp salad

You will need for 3-4 servings:
METRIC/IMPERIAL
1 medium-sized cauliflower
½ cucumber, cut into small dice
1 (198-g/7-oz) can peeled shrimps or prawns in brine

4 tablespoons mayonnaise (see page 87)
1 teaspoon lemon juice
pinch cayenne pepper

1 Wash the cauliflower and cut into small sprigs. Place in a pan in 2.5 cm/1 inch of boiling salted water.
2 Cover and simmer for 8-10 minutes or until just tender.
3 Drain and rinse in cold water.
4 Mix the cauliflower, diced cucumber and shrimps with the mayonnaise, lemon juice and cayenne pepper.
5 Place in a salad bowl and chill before serving.

Salade niçoise

You will need for 4 servings:
METRIC/IMPERIAL
3 tomatoes, skinned and quartered
½ cucumber, sliced
225 g/8 oz French beans, cooked and cut into 3-cm/1½-inch lengths
1 small green pepper, quartered, seeded and thinly sliced
1 small onion, finely chopped
1 cos lettuce, cut into 5-cm/2-inch strips
5 tablespoons French dressing (see page 86)

1 clove garlic, crushed
1 (198-g/7-oz) can tuna, drained and flaked
1 (56-g/2-oz) can anchovy fillets
50 g/2 oz stuffed green olives, sliced
2 hard-boiled eggs, peeled and halved
chopped parsley (optional)

1 Put tomatoes, cucumber, beans, green pepper and onion into a bowl.
2 Arrange prepared lettuce in the bottom of a salad bowl or serving dish.
3 Make the dressing (see page 86), add the crushed garlic and shake well.
4 Pour the dressing over the vegetables, mix thoroughly and then place them on top of the lettuce.
5 Toss lightly.
6 Arrange the anchovies, olives and eggs on top, and sprinkle with parsley if used.
7 Serve at once.

Tuna and pepper salad

You will need for 4 servings:
METRIC/IMPERIAL
1 medium-sized green pepper
1 red pepper
1 (198-g/7-oz) can tuna fish
50 g/2 oz black olives
1 (56-g/2-oz) can anchovies, drained

3 tablespoons French dressing (see page 86)
chopped parsley or chives

1 Cut the peppers in half and remove core, seeds and white pith.
2 Place the peppers, skin side up, under a hot grill and grill until the skin is black.
3 Peel off when cooled and cut the peppers into strips.
4 Drain the tuna and flake into a bowl.
5 Add the peppers, olives and the anchovies.
6 Pour over the French dressing. Toss lightly.
7 Serve sprinkled with parsley or chives.
8 Serve with a tomato salad. (See page 63.)
Variations:
1 Use cut green beans instead of the green pepper.
2 Use almond stuffed olives instead of black ones.

Cottage cheese and tuna salad

You will need for 3-4 servings:

METRIC/IMPERIAL

1 tablespoon chopped
  stuffed olives
1 tablespoon chopped
  parsley
2 carrots, grated
6 radishes, sliced
3 spring onions, sliced
1 tablespoon white
  vinegar or lemon
  juice

½ teaspoon
  Worcestershire
  sauce
seasoning
1 (198-g/7-oz) can
  tuna fish
225 g/8 oz cottage
  cheese
1 lettuce

1 Put the olives and parsley in a bowl with the carrots, radishes and spring onions.
2 Mix the vinegar, Worcestershire sauce and seasoning together.
3 Drain the oil from the tuna and flake the flesh.
4 Add the fish and cottage cheese to the salad ingredients, add the dressing and toss together lightly.
5 Line a salad bowl with a few of the lettuce leaves, shred remainder and place in the base.
6 Arrange the salad over the top.
7 Serve with brown bread and butter.

Variation:
For a heartier salad, use 2 tins of tuna fish and serve with an accompanying tomato salad.

Tuna and radish salad

You will need for 4 servings:

METRIC/IMPERIAL

100 g/4 oz long-grain
  rice
1 (198-g/7-oz) can
  tuna fish
2 tablespoons
  chopped parsley
2-3 dill cucumbers,
  diced
100 g/4 oz radishes,
  washed and thinly
  sliced

3 tablespoons French
  dressing (see page
  86)
to garnish:
2 tomatoes, sliced
2.5-cm/1-inch piece
  cucumber, thinly
  sliced
1 (56-g/2-oz) can
  anchovy fillets
parsley sprigs

1 Cook the rice in boiling salted water until just tender, 12-15 minutes, drain and refresh in cold water. Drain well and place in a bowl.
2 Drain the tuna and flake.
3 Add to the rice with the parsley, dill cucumbers, radishes and the French dressing. Toss well.
4 Arrange on a serving dish decorated with the sliced tomatoes and cucumber.
5 Drain the anchovies and dry on kitchen paper.
6 Arrange in a lattice over the salad. Decorate with sprigs of parsley.

Variation:
Garnish with hard-boiled eggs.

Peggy's salad

You will need for 4-5 servings:

METRIC/IMPERIAL

1 (198-g/7-oz) can
  tuna fish
100 g/4 oz radishes,
  washed
heart of a cos lettuce,
  washed
2.5-cm/1-inch piece
  cucumber

1 small or ½ yellow
  pepper
3 tablespoons French
  dressing (see page
  86)
to garnish:
2 hard-boiled eggs
chopped parsley

1 Drain and flake the tuna; place in a bowl.
2 Slice the radishes thinly and add.
3 Tear the lettuce into pieces and add.
4 Thinly slice the cucumber.
5 Remove core and seeds from the pepper; wash and slice thinly.
6 Add to the ingredients in the bowl.
7 Stir in the dressing just before serving.
8 Garnish with sliced eggs and sprinkle with chopped parsley.

Variations:
1 Add cooked cut French beans and quarters of tomato.
2 If yellow pepper is not available, use red or green but these need to be blanched. (Place sliced pepper in water and bring to the boil, drain and refresh with cold water.) Yellow peppers do not need blanching because they are sweeter.

Rollmop salad

You will need for 4 servings:

METRIC/IMPERIAL

450 g/1 lb new
  potatoes
salt
1 (350-g/12-oz) jar
  rollmop herrings
3 sticks celery
2 small red eating
  apples
juice of ½ lemon

3 tablespoons thick
  mayonnaise (see
  page 87)
bunch of watercress
pepper
paprika
to garnish:
cooked beetroot

1 Prepare the potatoes and cook in boiling salted water for 10-15 minutes until just tender.
2 Drain well, cool and slice.
3 Drain the herrings, cut into pieces and put in a bowl.
4 Wash and slice the celery.
5 Quarter the apples, remove the core and slice thinly; toss in the lemon juice.
6 Add the potatoes, celery, apples and mayonnaise to the fish.
7 Arrange the salad on a plate.
8 Wash the watercress and remove the long part of the stem.
9 Arrange the watercress round the edge of the fish.
10 Sprinkle with pepper and paprika.
11 Garnish with the cold cooked beetroot, diced, round the plate. Serve with brown bread.

Variations:

1 Make a dressing of 2 tablespoons soured cream and 1 tablespoon of mayonnaise instead of all mayonnaise.
2 Add dried basil to the mayonnaise.

Egg and cheese salads

Scandinavian egg and potato salad

You will need for 4 servings:

METRIC/IMPERIAL

450 g/1 lb new potatoes	2 sticks celery, washed and sliced
4 hard-boiled eggs	3-4 tablespoons mayonnaise (see page 87)
50 g/2 oz Danish Blue cheese	
1 large dill cucumber	1 tablespoon chopped parsley
175 g/6 oz onion, finely chopped	seasoning

1 Cook potatoes in boiling salted water until just tender. Cool quickly with cold water and peel off the skins.
2 Cut the potatoes into dice.
3 Remove eggs from their shells, chop two and slice two.
4 Chop the cucumber and crumble the cheese.
5 Mix the potatoes, chopped eggs, cheese, cucumber, onion, celery, mayonnaise, seasoning and some of the parsley gently together, being careful not to break up the potatoes.
6 Place in a serving dish, garnish with the sliced egg and sprinkle with the remaining parsley.

Variation:

Diced beetroot is also a good garnish, but put on just before serving.

Curried egg salad

You will need for 4 servings:

METRIC/IMPERIAL

25 g/1 oz butter or margarine	1 canned red pimiento
1 medium-sized onion, chopped	1 green eating apple
	seasoning
1½ tablespoons curry powder	4 large hard-boiled eggs
175 g/6 oz long-grain rice	Curried mayonnaise (see page 87)
450-600 ml/¾-1 pint stock	*to garnish:*
	paprika
	watercress

1 Place the butter or margarine in a saucepan with the onion.
2 Cook for 10 minutes without browning.
3 Add the curry powder and cook for 5 minutes, stirring occasionally.
4 Add the rice, stir and cook until opaque, about 3 minutes.
5 Stir in 450 ml/¾ pint of the stock and cook for 12-15 minutes until tender, or until the stock has been absorbed. If necessary, add the remaining stock.
6 When cooked, drain well and arrange on a serving plate to cool.
7 Cut the pimiento and apple into slices and stir into the cooled rice with seasoning to taste.
8 Cut the eggs in half and arrange cut side down on the rice.
9 Spoon the mayonnaise over the eggs.
10 Sprinkle the eggs with a little paprika and garnish with the watercress.

Courgette and egg mayonnaise

You will need for 4 servings:

METRIC/IMPERIAL

350 g/12 oz small courgettes	8 hard-boiled eggs
4 medium-sized tomatoes	6 tablespoons mayonnaise (see page 87)
50 g/2 oz button mushrooms, washed and sliced	3 tablespoons single cream
4 tablespoons French dressing (see page 86)	1 tablespoon chopped parsley
	2 teaspoons chopped chives
1 small lettuce	

1 Wash the courgettes and cut into thick matchsticks.
2 Bring a pan of salted water to the boil, add the courgettes and cook for 2 minutes.
3 Drain well and refresh under cold water.
4 Skin the tomatoes by placing in boiling water. Leave for a count of about 10 then remove the skins.
5 Cut the tomatoes into quarters and remove the seeds, cut each piece in half.
6 Place in a bowl with the courgettes, add the mushrooms.
7 Pour over the dressing and leave to chill for about 1 hour.
8 Wash and shred the lettuce and arrange on a round dish.
9 Pile the salad in the centre.
10 Cut the eggs in half lengthwise and arrange round the edge of the plate.
11 Mix the mayonnaise, cream, parsley and chives together and spoon over the eggs.

Mum's 8 layer salad

You will need for 6 servings:
METRIC/IMPERIAL

225 g/8 oz fresh
  spinach, washed
  thoroughly
1 cos lettuce heart,
  washed
175 g/6 oz red
  cabbage, finely
  chopped
1 bunch spring
  onions, trimmed
  and washed
2 hard-boiled eggs,
  peeled
75 g/3 oz Cheddar
  cheese, grated

100 g/4 oz frozen petit
  pois, thawed
for the dressing:
2 tablespoons
  mayonnaise (see
  page 87)
2 tablespoons natural
  yoghurt
2 tablespoons soured
  cream
1 tablespoon white
  wine vinegar
1 tablespoon water
pinch sugar
seasoning

1 Finely shred the spinach and arrange in a layer in a fairly straight sided glass dish.
2 Shred the lettuce and arrange this in a layer in the dish.
3 Cover lettuce with the red cabbage.
4 Thinly slice the spring onions and sprinkle over the cabbage.
5 Chop the hard-boiled eggs and sprinkle over.
6 Arrange the Cheddar cheese in a ring round the edge.
7 Place the peas in the centre. Chill.
8 Make the dressing by mixing all the ingredients together; pour evenly over the salad just before serving.
9 Serve with cold meats.

Greek salad

You will need for 3-4 servings:
METRIC/IMPERIAL

¼ cucumber
225 g/8 oz tomatoes
1 medium-sized green
  pepper
1 medium Spanish
  onion

4 tablespoons French
  dressing (see page
  86)
175 g/6 oz Feta cheese

1 Thinly slice the cucumber and place in a bowl.
2 Wash the tomatoes, cut into quarters and add.
3 Wash, remove seeds and core from the pepper, cut into thin strips and add.
4 Peel the onion and slice thinly; add to the bowl.
5 Toss in the dressing.
6 Cut the cheese into cubes and mix into the salad.
7 Serve well chilled with French bread.
Variations:
1 Sprinkle with 1 teaspoon of dried marjoram or 2 teaspoons if using chopped fresh.
2 Crumble the cheese into the dressing and toss.
3 To extend the salad, although not authentic, add some torn cos lettuce.

Tomato and cheese salad ring

You will need for 6-8 servings:
METRIC/IMPERIAL

450 g/1 lb tomatoes
350 g/12 oz cottage
  cheese
seasoning
10-cm/4-inch length
  cucumber

225 g/8 oz red
  Leicester cheese,
  finely grated
to garnish:
watercress

1 Lightly brush an 18-cm/7-inch ring mould with oil.
2 Cut the tomatoes into slices and arrange six in the base of the mould.
3 Place cottage cheese in a bowl and season with the salt and pepper.
4 Spread evenly over the sliced tomatoes and press down well.
5 Dice the cucumber and arrange over the cottage cheese.
6 Arrange the remaining tomato slices over the cucumber.
7 Spread the grated cheese over the cucumber, press down firmly.
8 Leave in the refrigerator for about 1 hour before turning out.
9 Loosen the sides carefully, place a serving plate on top, invert and shake out of the mould.
10 Garnish with watercress.
11 Serve with a tossed salad, brown bread and butter.
Variations:
1 Add chopped fresh chives to the cottage cheese.
2 Use a mixture of Caerphilly and Danish blue cheese instead of the red Leicester.
3 Use cottage cheese with pineapple added and mix with a little chopped ham.
4 Fill the centre with chopped celery and cold cooked peas.

Chicory and cheese salad

You will need for 2 servings:
METRIC/IMPERIAL

1 large head chicory
100 g/4 oz grated
  Cheddar cheese
40 g/1½ oz sultanas,
  washed and
  drained
100 g/4 oz black or
  green grapes,
  seeded

1 teaspoon lemon
  juice
4 teaspoons corn oil
seasoning
2 tablespoons
  chopped parsley

1 Trim and wash the chicory, drain well on kitchen paper and cut into thick slices, place in a bowl.
2 Add the cheese, sultanas and grapes to the chicory.
3 Mix the lemon juice, oil and seasoning together and pour over the salad.
4 Toss lightly and serve in a bowl or individual plates.
5 Sprinkle with parsley.
Variation:
Use lettuce and celery instead of the chicory.

Vegetable salads

Artichoke salad

You will need for 4 servings:

METRIC/IMPERIAL
juice of ½ lemon
2 tablespoons port
2 tablespoons salad
  oil
pinch sugar
¼ teaspoon mustard
seasoning

100 g/4 oz button
  mushrooms
350 g/12 oz Jerusalem
  artichokes
2 spring onions
1 tablespoon chopped
  parsley

1 In a screw-topped jar, mix together the lemon juice, port, oil, sugar, mustard and seasoning. Shake thoroughly.
2 Lightly wash or wipe the mushrooms and slice thinly. Place in a bowl with the prepared dressing.
3 Wash and peel the artichokes, then slice thinly and add to the mushrooms. Toss well in the dressing to prevent the artichokes from discolouring.
4 Wash and trim the onions, slice thinly and add to the salad together with the parsley.
5 Serve immediately.

Variation:
Add 1 tablespoon grated Parmesan cheese to the dressing and add 1 tablespoon raisins to the salad.

Aubergine and mushroom salad

You will need for 4-6 servings:

METRIC/IMPERIAL
450 g/1 lb aubergines
salt
225 g/8 oz
  mushrooms
8 tablespoons oil
2 tablespoons wine
  vinegar

pepper
chopped parsley

1 Prepare and slice the aubergines; cut the slices in half if large.
2 Spread slices on absorbent paper, sprinkle with salt and leave 30 minutes.
3 Rinse and dry them.
4 Wipe and slice the mushrooms.
5 Heat the oil in a frying pan and cook aubergines for 10-15 minutes until softening.
6 Stir in the vinegar, mushrooms and seasoning. Continue cooking fairly quickly to soften the mushrooms without allowing too much juice to drain out.
7 Leave until cold and serve sprinkled generously with the parsley.

Avocado and grapefruit salad

You will need for 4 servings:

METRIC/IMPERIAL
1 or 2 avocado pears
1 grapefruit
other salad
  vegetables, e.g.
  tomato, watercress,
  endive, green
  pepper

for the dressing:
6 tablespoons corn oil
3 tablespoons vinegar
1 tablespoon sugar
seasoning

1 Cut peeled avocado pears into slices, remove stones, and divide the peeled grapefruit into sections.
2 Prepare the selected salad vegetables.
3 Thoroughly combine all the ingredients for the dressing then toss the salad in the dressing.

Beansprout salad

You will need for 4 servings:

METRIC/IMPERIAL
for the sauce:
4 tablespoons corn oil
2 tablespoons lemon
  juice or cider
  vinegar
2 tablespoons soy
  sauce
¼ teaspoon salt
1 medium onion,
  finely chopped
2 tablespoons toasted
  sesame seeds

1 clove garlic, crushed
1 tablespoon chopped
  chives
2 tablespoons
  chopped parsley
⅛ teaspoon grated
  fresh ginger root
  (optional)
for the salad:
225 g/8 oz fresh bean
  sprouts

1 Mix all the sauce ingredients together.
2 Wash the beansprouts and drain well.
3 Place the beansprouts in a serving dish and pour the dressing over.
4 Toss lightly and chill well before serving.

Broad bean and potato salad

You will need for 4 servings:

METRIC/IMPERIAL
450 g/1 lb new
  potatoes, small
1 kg/2 lb broad beans
75 g/3 oz butter
100 g/4 oz streaky
  bacon

to garnish:
chopped parsley
  (optional)

1 Scrape the potatoes and cook in boiling salted water until tender, about 15 minutes depending on size.
2 Shell the beans and cook in boiling salted water until just tender.
3 Melt the butter in a pan. Remove the rind from the bacon, chop and add to the butter. Stir over gentle heat until cooked but not browned.
4 Add the drained potatoes and broad beans. Toss well and serve immediately. If liked, sprinkle with chopped parsley.

Carrot and watercress salad

You will need for 4 servings:

METRIC/IMPERIAL

6 slices bread	seasoning
2 tablespoons oil	1 clove garlic, crushed
50 g/2 oz butter	4 tablespoons salad
225 g/8 oz carrots	oil
2 bunches watercress	*to garnish:*
1 orange	slices of orange
for the dressing:	
½ teaspoon sugar	

1 Remove the crusts from the bread and cut it into small cubes.
2 Heat the oil and butter together in a pan, then add the bread and fry until golden. Drain on kitchen paper.
3 Peel or scrub the carrots and grate them.
4 Wash the watercress, dry and remove the stalks.
5 Toss the carrot and watercress together.
6 To make the dressing, grate the rind from the orange and mix with the juice.
7 Add the sugar, seasoning, garlic and oil.
8 Stir or shake together well until completely emulsified then pour over the carrot mixture and toss well.
9 Serve surrounded by the croûtons and garnish with slices of orange.

Variation:
Add a little coarsely grated Danish blue cheese.

Carrot tomato date salad

You will need for 4 servings:

METRIC/IMPERIAL

225 g/8 oz tomatoes	½ teaspoon basil
2 tablespoons oil	350 g/12 oz carrots
2 tablespoons vinegar	25 g/1 oz dates
seasoning	

1 Concasser the tomatoes, reserving the seeds and juice (see page 63). Cut flesh into strips and drain on kitchen paper.
2 Put seeds and juice into pan with the oil, vinegar, seasoning and basil.
3 Boil 3-4 minutes until thick and syrupy, making about 2 tablespoons.
4 Strain, rubbing juices through the strainer into a bowl.
5 Peel and grate the raw carrots.
6 Chop the dates and mix them with the carrots, tomato strips and juices.
7 Add more seasoning if needed.

Carrot ring mould

You will need for 8-10 servings:

METRIC/IMPERIAL

1 kg/2 lb new carrots, scraped and thickly sliced	100 g/4 oz frozen peas, cooked and cooled
25 g/1 oz butter	2 sticks celery, chopped into 1-cm/½-inch pieces
150 ml/¼ pint chicken stock	4 tablespoons thin mayonnaise (see page 87)
1 tablespoon sugar	seasoning
seasoning	*to garnish:*
15 g/½ oz gelatine	chopped parsley
3 eggs, separated	
grated rind and juice of ½ lemon	
50 g/2 oz grated Cheddar cheese	
for the filling:	
100 g/4 oz button onions, peeled and left whole	
75 ml/3 fl oz chicken stock	
seasoning	
½ bay leaf	

1 Place the carrots in cold salted water, bring to the boil and simmer for 2 minutes.
2 Drain well, then place in pan with the butter, stock, sugar and seasoning to taste and cook gently until carrots are very tender and have absorbed the liquid.
3 Meanwhile, dissolve the gelatine in a bowl with a little hot water, over a pan of boiling water.
4 Mash the carrots finely, or blend in a liquidiser.
5 Mix the carrot purée with the egg yolks, lemon rind and juice, grated cheese and dissolved gelatine, and combine weil.
6 Season to taste again if required and leave to cool.
7 Whisk the egg whites until very stiff and carefully fold into the cooled carrot mixture.
8 Mix well and spoon into a wetted 1.25-litre/2-pint ring mould.
9 Level off the surface and leave in refrigerator to set.
10 To prepare the filling, poach the onions in a little extra stock with seasoning and bay leaf until just tender.
11 Drain and place in cold water. Cook the peas in boiling salted water and drain.
12 Mix the cooked peas, onions and celery pieces.
13 Add mayonnaise and coat well, adding seasoning to taste.
14 When mould is set, turn out onto serving plate and fill the centre with the vegetable mayonnaise filling.
15 Serve sprinkled with chopped parsley.

Variations:
1 Replace the peas with frozen mixed vegetables for a colourful filling.
2 Cut up sliced ham into matchstick lengths and add to the vegetables in the centre.
3 Add fresh herbs or chives to the mayonnaise.

Chinese cabbage and celery salad

You will need for 8 servings:

METRIC/IMPERIAL

1 head Chinese
  cabbage, trimmed
  and washed
½ head celery,
  trimmed and
  washed
2 large red canned
  pimientos, cut into
  strips

10 black olives
150 ml/¼ pint French
  dressing or
  mayonnaise (see
  pages 86 and 87)

1 Chop the cabbage finely and slice the celery into 1-cm/½-inch pieces.
2 Mix together and add the strips of pimiento and black olives.
3 Serve tossed in the French dressing or mayonnaise.

Red cabbage

You will need for 4 servings:

METRIC/IMPERIAL

450 g/1 lb red
  cabbage
50 g/2 oz butter
1 large Spanish onion,
  thinly sliced

4 tablespoons
  blackcurrant juice
seasoning

1 Wash and quarter the cabbage, remove any damaged outside leaves.
2 Remove core and shred cabbage finely.
3 Melt the butter in a medium saucepan, preferably non-stick.
4 Add the cabbage and onion to the pan, toss in the melted butter and seasoning.
5 Add the blackcurrant juice.
6 Cover and cook very gently, stirring frequently so the cabbage does not catch.
7 Cook for 25-30 minutes until just tender.
8 Serve either hot or cold.

Note:

The blackcurrant juice helps to keep the colour of the cabbage and adds an extra richness to the flavour.

Red cabbage coleslaw

You will need for 10-12 servings:

METRIC/IMPERIAL

1 kg/2 lb red cabbage
2 large onions
1 teaspoon celery
  seed
225 g/8 oz sugar
seasoning
for the dressing:
1 teaspoon pepper

1 teaspoon dry
  mustard
300 ml/½ pint white
  wine vinegar
300 ml/½ pint corn oil

1 Discard the coarse outer leaves of the cabbage.
2 Cut into quarters, remove core and shred cabbage finely.
3 Peel and thinly slice the onions.
4 Place these in a large bowl; sprinkle with celery seed, sugar and a little seasoning.
5 To make the dressing, blend the pepper and mustard together and place in a saucepan with the vinegar. Bring quickly to the boil.
6 Add the corn oil, mix together and pour over the cabbage.
7 Toss the cabbage in the dressing.
8 Leave to stand for 1 day before serving, stirring occasionally.

Note:

1 This will keep for weeks in a covered container.
2 The cabbage and onion could be chopped rather than sliced.

Red coleslaw with celery

You will need for 8 servings:

METRIC/IMPERIAL

1 small head red
  cabbage
2 large oranges
½ head celery

50 g/2 oz walnut
  halves
lemon or orange juice
seasoning

1 Wash and trim the cabbage; shred finely.
2 Using a sharp knife, cut off rind and pith from the oranges; cut in between the membrane to remove the segments.
3 Chop the celery into 2.5-cm/1-inch pieces and mix with the oranges, cabbage and walnuts. Toss in the lemon or orange juice and season to taste.

Variations:

1 Use salted peanuts instead of walnuts.
2 Chop a small onion very finely and mix in.
3 Omit lemon juice, make a vinaigrette with orange juice, pour over and leave to marinate.
4 Use blackcurrant juice in a vinaigrette. The flavour goes well with red cabbage.

Moya's winter salad

You will need for 6 servings:

METRIC/IMPERIAL

450 g/1 lb red
  cabbage
1 medium-sized leek,
  trimmed
175 g/6 oz carrots,
  peeled
50 g/2 oz seedless
  raisins
50 g/2 oz salted
  peanuts

2 tablespoons
  mayonnaise (see
  page 87)
1 (142-ml/5-fl oz)
  carton soured
  cream
seasoning

1 Remove the outer leaves from the cabbage, cut cabbage in quarters and remove hard core.

2 Finely shred the cabbage, place in large bowl.

3 Thoroughly wash the leek to remove any grit, cut across in thin slices and add to the cabbage.

4 Coarsely grate the carrots and add to the cabbage with the raisins and peanuts.

5 Mix the mayonnaise and soured cream together with seasoning.

6 Add to the salad just before serving and toss lightly and arrange in a salad bowl.

7 Serve with brown bread and butter. This salad goes well with hard-boiled eggs.

Variations

1 Use finely chopped onion instead of leek.

2 Crumble in some Caerphilly cheese for extra nourishment.

3 Add cooked soya beans for a really hearty salad.

Spanish salata

You will need for 4 servings:

METRIC/IMPERIAL

450 g/1 lb white cabbage, finely shredded	100 g/4 oz whole green beans, cooked and cooled
6 tablespoons mayonnaise (see page 87)	2 hard-boiled eggs, sliced
1 tablespoon chopped capers	50 g/2 oz stuffed green olives, chopped
2 small cooked beetroot, diced	seasoning

1 Mix together the cabbage, mayonnaise and capers.

2 Spread over the base of a serving dish, preferably oblong or oval.

3 Arrange the beetroot in two lines, one at each end of the dish.

4 Put two lines of green beans, then the sliced eggs, and one central line of olives.

5 Sprinkle with seasoning and serve chilled.

Fruity coleslaw

You will need for 4 servings:

METRIC/IMPERIAL

350 g/12 oz white cabbage	grated rind of 1 lemon
100 g/4 oz new carrots	4 tablespoons mayonnaise (see page 87)
4 spring onions	seasoning
1 small green pepper	
2 small red crisp eating apples or Cox's	

1 Discard coarse outer leaves and thick stalk from the cabbage. Shred cabbage finely, put in a bowl.

2 Scrape carrots and grate coarsely; add to the cabbage.

3 Trim off the ends from the onions and discard; slice onions thinly.

4 Wash peppers, remove core and seeds, dice the flesh and add to the cabbage with the onion.

5 Quarter the apples, remove core and dice the apple; add to the bowl with the remaining ingredients.

6 Stir to mix evenly and arrange in a serving dish.

Coleslaw salad ring

You will need for 6 servings:

METRIC/IMPERIAL

300 ml/½ pint vegetable stock (or water and stock cube)	175 g/6 oz fresh or frozen sweetcorn kernels
15 g/½ oz gelatine	8 tablespoons mayonnaise (see page 87)
1 small white cabbage	seasoning
1 green pepper	cress or parsley
3 carrots	

1 Place 150 ml/¼ pint of the stock in a small bowl, sprinkle over the gelatine.

2 Place the bowl over a saucepan filled with hot water. Stir to dissolve, remove the bowl from the heat and pour over the remaining stock. Leave to become cold.

3 Remove the tough outer leaves from the cabbage and finely shred the remainder.

4 Rinse the cabbage and dry thoroughly. Place in a bowl.

5 Wash the pepper and remove core, white pith and the seeds. Slice very thinly.

6 Peel and coarsely grate the carrots; add to the cabbage with the peppers.

7 Cook the sweetcorn in boiling salted water for 5-7 minutes. Drain and refresh under cold water.

8 Add the sweetcorn to the salad.

9 Stir in the mayonnaise, add the seasoning and the gelatine which should be nearly on the point of setting.

11 Leave in a cold place to set.

12 When set, loosen the salad ring and turn out onto a dish.

13 Fill the centre with either cress or parsley.

Cauliflower salad

You will need for 4-6 servings:

METRIC/IMPERIAL

½ medium-sized cauliflower	50 g/2 oz button mushrooms, washed (optional)
100 g/4 oz carrots	Blue cheese sauce (see page 88)
50 g/2 oz sultanas	
small lettuce	

1 Trim the cauliflower, removing the hard stalk. Divide into florets and place in a bowl.

2 Peel and coarsely grate the carrots and add to the bowl with the sultanas.

3 Wash the lettuce, remove the green outer leaves and reserve. Shred the remainder and add to the salad.

4 Toss lightly with the mushrooms, if used.

5 Arrange the reserved leaves round the sides of a shallow glass bowl and fill the centre with the salad.

6 Serve with Blue cheese sauce.

Variations:

1 Add 100 g/4 oz shredded red cabbage.

2 Serve with slices or cubes of salami tossed into the salad.

Celery salad

You will need for 8 servings:

METRIC/IMPERIAL

175 g/6 oz brown rice	chopped parsley
salt	4 medium-sized
4 sticks celery,	tomatoes, halved in
washed and diced	a waterlily shape
50 g/2 oz raisins	4 hard-boiled eggs,
fresh herbs, finely	halved lengthways
chopped (as	150 ml/¼ pint thick
available)	mayonnaise (see
50 g/2 oz green	page 87)
grapes	8 black olives
seasoning	

1 Cook the brown rice in boiling salted water according to directions on the packet – about 45 minutes until just tender.

2 Rinse well, drain and leave to cool.

3 When cold, mix with the diced celery, raisins, chopped herbs, grapes and seasoning.

4 Pile into the centre of the serving dish and sprinkle with chopped parsley.

5 Arrange halves of tomato and egg alternately round the edge of the dish.

6 Place the mayonnaise in a piping bag and decorate the egg halves.

7 Decorate each halved tomato with a black olive.

Celery, carrot and mushroom salad

You will need for 6 servings:

METRIC/IMPERIAL

1 head celery, washed	50 g/2 oz sultanas
175 g/6 oz carrots	1 tablespoon parsley
100 g/4 oz button	or chives, chopped
mushrooms,	3 tablespoons French
washed	dressing (see page
50 g/2 oz peanuts	86)

1 Slice the celery finely and place in a bowl.

2 Grate the carrots coarsely and add.

3 Slice the mushrooms and chop the peanuts and add to the celery with the sultanas.

4 Stir in the parsley and dressing.

5 Serve with cottage cheese and hard-boiled eggs.

Variation:

Use Sour cream and mayonnaise dressing (see page 87) instead of French dressing.

Chicory and leek salad

You will need for 3-4 servings:

METRIC/IMPERIAL

225 g/8 oz chicory	5 tablespoons corn oil
2 medium-sized leeks	2 tablespoons orange
225 g/8 oz tomatoes	juice
pinch each salt,	1 tablespoon white
pepper, castor	wine vinegar
sugar	chopped parsley
½ teaspoon dry	
mustard	

1 Remove the outside leaves of the chicory if necessary. Wash and cut into pieces and place in a bowl.

2 Trim off the green foliage from the leeks and discard or use for soup.

3 Wash the leeks thoroughly to remove all grit, especially in the layers.

4 Cut the leeks into thin slices and add to the chicory.

5 Skin, quarter and remove the seeds from the tomatoes; add to the leeks, etc.

6 Place the seasonings in a bowl with the mustard, blend in the oil and gradually whisk in the orange juice and vinegar. Mix well.

7 Toss the vegetables in the dressing.

8 Sprinkle over the chopped parsley just before serving.

Variation:

Use apple juice instead of orange juice and a little chopped fresh mint instead of parsley.

Orange and chicory salad

You will need for 4 servings:

METRIC/IMPERIAL

225 g/8 oz chicory	4 tablespoons French
1 orange	dressing (see page 86)
50 g/2 oz seedless	1 tablespoon chopped
raisins	parsley

1 Wash the chicory, removing any damaged outside leaves and, using a stainless knife, cut the chicory into fairly thin slices.

2 Place in a bowl.

3 Using a sharp knife, cut the rind and pith off the orange and cut out the segments.

4 Add these to the salad with the remaining ingredients.

Courgette salad

You will need for 4 servings:

METRIC/IMPERIAL

1 red pepper, sliced	½ head celery, diced
into strips	Lemon-flavoured
1 medium-sized	French dressing
onion, thinly sliced	(see page 86)
225 g/8 oz courgettes,	
cut into thick chunks	

1 Wash all the vegetables and prepare.
2 Place all in a large pan of salted water and bring to the boil.
3 Drain and quickly refresh under cold water. Dry on kitchen paper.
4 Arrange in a salad bowl, and pour the dressing over and toss lightly.
5 Chill before serving.

Courgette and orange salad

You will need for 4 servings:

METRIC/IMPERIAL

225 g/8 oz courgettes	2 tablespoons corn oil
2 small oranges	1 tablespoon cider
for the dressing:	vinegar
pinch each salt and	*to garnish:*
dry mustard	little chopped parsley
¼ teaspoon each	
ground mace or	
allspice and castor	
sugar	

1 Trim the ends from the courgettes and wash; cut into fairly thin slices.
2 Put in a pan of salted water, bring to the boil and cook for 2 minutes. Drain and refresh under cold water, drain well.
3 Using a sharp knife, remove the rind and pith from the oranges and cut out the segments.
4 Place the courgettes and orange in a serving dish. Chill well before serving.
5 Place the dressing ingredients in a screw-top jar. Shake well and pour over the salad just before serving.
6 Sprinkle with chopped parsley.

Pickled cucumber salad

You will need for 4-6 servings:

METRIC/IMPERIAL

1 large cucumber	½ teaspoon salt
2 teaspoons salt	pinch pepper
3 tablespoons white	1 tablespoon chopped
vinegar	fresh dill
15 g/½ oz castor sugar	

1 Wash the cucumber, trim the ends and score the cucumber lengthways with a fork.
2 Slice cucumber very thinly, place in a bowl and sprinkle with the 2 teaspoons salt. Leave for several hours.
3 Press the juice out of the cucumber and drain on kitchen paper.
4 Place cucumber in a dish.
5 Blend the remaining ingredients together except the dill; pour over the cucumber. Sprinkle with the dill just before serving.

Sweet and sour cucumber

You will need for 6 servings:

METRIC/IMPERIAL

1 cucumber	75 g/3 oz castor sugar
2 teaspoons salt	½ teaspoon pepper
3 tablespoons water	chopped fresh dill
2 tablespoons white	(optional)
wine vinegar	

1 Wash the cucumber, trim each end and score the length of the cucumber with a fork. Slice thinly, place in a bowl and sprinkle with the salt.
2 Allow to stand for about an hour so that the juices are released from the cucumber.
3 Drain well, pressing with a saucer to remove excess liquid.
4 Make up the dressing with the water, vinegar, sugar and pepper. Mix well.
5 Pour over the cucumber and allow to chill before serving. Sprinkle with chopped fresh dill, if used.

Leek and tomato vinaigrette

You will need for 6 servings:

METRIC/IMPERIAL

1.5 kg/3 lb leeks	150 ml/¼ pint French
salt	dressing (see page
3 large tomatoes	86)

1 Thoroughly wash the leeks and trim off the extra green and the roots.
2 Cut the leeks into 5-cm/2-inch slices and wash again to remove any possible trace of grit between the leaves.
3 Place about 2.5 cm/1 inch of water in a pan.
4 Add the leeks, bring to the boil and cook for 3-5 minutes, shaking the pan once. The thicker root pieces will take longer but the leeks should still be slightly crisp.
5 Drain the leeks very well and leave them for about 5 minutes while preparing the tomatoes.
6 Cover the tomatoes with boiling water and leave for about 10 seconds.
7 Peel off the skins, cut into quarters and remove the seeds.
8 Chop the flesh into large dice.
9 Place the still warm leeks in a serving dish and pour over the dressing. Leave to become cold, turning them occasionally.
10 Just before serving, sprinkle with the prepared tomatoes. Serve cold but not chilled.
Variations:
1 Cook the leeks for even less time or leave raw.
2 Sprinkle with plenty of parsley and freshly ground pepper just before serving.

Leek and mushroom salad

You will need for 3-4 servings:

METRIC/IMPERIAL
6 small leeks
salt
175 g/6 oz button
   mushrooms

French dressing (see
   page 86)
2 tablespoons
   chopped parsley

1 Trim the outer leaves and ends from the leeks.
2 Wash leeks well in cold water.
3 Cut into 5-cm/2-inch diagonal pieces.
4 Cook in a little boiling salted water for 5 minutes until just tender but still a little crisp. Drain well.
5 Wash and slice the mushrooms; mix with the leeks.
6 Add the dressing with the chopped parsley and leave to become cold.

Pea salad

You will need for 4-6 servings:

METRIC/IMPERIAL
350 g/12 oz frozen
   peas
100 g/4 oz button
   mushrooms
2 stalks celery
25 g/1 oz sultanas
½ small red pepper
   (optional)
3 tablespoons corn oil

1 tablespoon white
   wine vinegar
seasoning
¼ teaspoon dry
   mustard
1 teaspoon castor
   sugar
1 clove garlic, crushed

1 Cook the peas according to the given directions. Drain and refresh under cold water.
2 Place in a salad bowl.
3 Wash and thinly slice the mushrooms and celery.
4 Add to the peas with the sultanas.
5 Cut the pepper into strips, if used, put in cold water, bring to the boil and refresh with cold water. Add to the salad and chill.
6 Place the remaining ingredients in a screw-top jar and shake well to mix.
7 Pour over the salad just before serving.
Variations:
1 Add chopped spring onions or chives.
2 Rub the bowl with a clove of garlic.
3 Add a small tin or packet of sweetcorn instead of using the sultanas.

French style pea salad

You will need for 4 servings:

METRIC/IMPERIAL
1 kg/2 lb fresh peas or
   450 g/1 lb shelled
   peas
sprig of fresh mint
salt
clove garlic (optional)
3 cos lettuce leaves,
   washed

3 large spring onions,
   trimmed to the
   white part
chopped parsley
   (optional)
3 tablespoons Mint
   vinaigrette (see page
   87)

1 Cook the peas with the mint in boiling salted water for 15-20 minutes, depending on the tenderness of the peas.
2 Remove the mint and strain the peas in a colander. Refresh under cold water.
3 Peel the garlic and rub around a wooden salad bowl.
4 Add the peas, tear the lettuce in pieces and add.
5 Slice the spring onions thinly and add to the peas, with the parsley if used. Chill until required.
6 Toss in the dressing just before serving.

Green pea and orange salad

You will need for 4-5 servings:

METRIC/IMPERIAL
225 g/8 oz cold
   cooked peas
25 g/1 oz Brazil nuts,
   chopped
25 g/1 oz sultanas
2 large oranges

3 sticks celery, sliced
3 tablespoons French
   dressing (see page
   86)
2 tablespoons
   chopped parsley

1 Place peas, nuts and sultanas in a bowl.
2 Using a sharp knife, remove the rind and pith from the oranges and cut the segments out from between the membranes.
3 Add to the bowl with the remaining ingredients.
4 Toss lightly and serve with cold roast duck.
Variations:
1 Use a small head of Chinese cabbage leaves instead of the celery.
2 Add two bunches of watercress, washed and sprigged, for extra colour.

Pepper and olive salad

You will need for 4 servings:

METRIC/IMPERIAL
1 large red pepper
1 large green pepper
150 ml/¼ pint olive oil
seasoning

3 cloves garlic, finely
   chopped
18 stuffed olives
chopped parsley

1 Wash peppers, halve, and remove core, seeds and pith.
2 Remove skin from peppers by placing under a grill. Cook until skin blisters and remove skin under a tap.
3 Cut flesh into large dice.
4 Place the oil in a frying pan with the peppers, seasoning and garlic.
5 Cover with a plate and cook *very slowly* for 15 minutes, turning occasionally.
6 Turn into a serving dish with the oil. Allow to cool.
7 Slice the olives and add with the chopped parsley. Serve well chilled.

Potato salad

You will need for 6 servings:

METRIC/IMPERIAL
1 kg/2 lb waxy new
  potatoes
salt
4 spring onions
3 generous
  tablespoons thick
  mayonnaise (see
  page 87)

1 tablespoon chopped
  parsley

1 Wash the potatoes and cook with their skins on in boiling salted water until just tender, about 15-20 minutes depending on size. Test with a sharp pointed knife.
2 Drain, refresh in cold water; peel off skins as soon as possible.
3 If small, keep whole, otherwise cut into slices.
4 Place in a bowl.
5 Prepare and thinly slice spring onions.
6 Add to the potatoes with the mayonnaise.
7 Toss lightly and turn into a clean bowl.
8 Sprinkle with parsley.
Variations:
1 Omit spring onions. Coarsely chop two hard-boiled eggs and two dill cucumbers. Add to the salad with the mayonnaise. Serve sprinkled with parsley.
2 Cook potatoes as in recipe but toss in a French dressing while still hot. The potatoes may be peeled or unpeeled.
3 Toss hot peeled new potatoes in a boiled salad dressing (see Red cabbage coleslaw page 76).

Hot potato salad

You will need for 4 servings:

METRIC/IMPERIAL
450 g/1 lb new
  potatoes
25 g/1 oz butter
2 medium-sized
  onions, thinly sliced
4 tablespoons water
4 tablespoons white
  wine vinegar

½ level teaspoon salt
freshly ground black
  pepper
1 tablespoon sugar
chopped parsley or
  fresh herbs
  (optional)

1 Cook the potatoes in their skins for about 15 minutes until just tender. Drain and peel off skins. Slice the potatoes.
2 Melt the butter in a fairly large saucepan, add the onions, cover and cook gently until soft without browning, about 10 minutes.
3 Add the remaining ingredients (except potatoes) and cook if necessary to soften the onion further.
4 Add the potatoes and heat through gently. Sprinkle with parsley or herbs if used.

Spinach salad

You will need for 4 servings:

METRIC/IMPERIAL
225 g/8 oz fresh
  spinach
1 carrot, grated
8-cm/3-inch length
  cucumber

4 tomatoes
1 orange
3 tablespoons French
  dressing (see page
  86)

1 Cut off thick stems from the spinach and wash the leaves very thoroughly.
2 Tear into pieces and place in a salad bowl with the carrot.
3 Wash the cucumber and cut into dice.
4 Wash the tomatoes and cut into thin wedges. Add these to the bowl with the cucumber.
5 Using a sharp knife, cut the rind and pith from the orange.
6 Cut out the segments and add to the salad.
7 Sprinkle over the dressing and toss the salad lightly.
Variation:
Add a little horseradish sauce to the dressing.

Tomatoes with sour cream relish

You will need for 4 servings:

METRIC/IMPERIAL
8 medium-sized
  tomatoes
double recipe of
  French dressing
  (see page 86)
2.5-cm/1-inch piece of
  cucumber, finely
  chopped

2 teaspoons creamed
  horseradish sauce
1 (142-ml/5-fl oz)
  carton soured
  cream
to garnish:
few mint leaves

1 Skin the tomatoes (A-Z Salad Vegetables, see page 63).
2 Either slice the tomatoes or leave whole.
3 Mix the French dressing, cucumber, horseradish and soured cream together.
4 Spoon over the tomatoes and decorate with the mint leaves.
5 Serve well chilled as a starter or side salad.
Variations:
1 Omit the cucumber and add chopped chives or parsley.
2 Serve the same sauce over small cooked baby beetroots instead of tomatoes.

Basque salad

You will need for 4 servings:

METRIC/IMPERIAL
2 red peppers
2-3 tablespoons oil
1 garlic clove, crushed
2 tablespoons red
  wine
½ teaspoon paprika

salt
½ teaspoon sugar
450 g/1 lb tomatoes,
  skinned
to garnish:
chopped parsley

1 Remove stalk and seeds from peppers.
2 Wipe and slice into strips.
3 Cook slowly in the oil with the garlic in a covered pan for about 45 minutes, until quite soft.
4 Mix in the wine, paprika, salt and sugar and increase the heat until bubbling.
5 Add tomatoes and cook for 5 minutes.
6 Leave until cold and serve sprinkled with chopped parsley.

Variation:
Use green peppers and green tomatoes with onion and white wine – omit garlic.

Apple and olive salad

You will need for 4 servings:
METRIC/IMPERIAL

2 eating apples	3 tablespoons French
1 tablespoon lemon	dressing (see page
juice	86)
10-12 stuffed olives	lettuce
6 radishes, sliced	
1 small green pepper, seeded and finely chopped	

1 Core and finely chop the apples, then toss in the lemon juice.
2 Add the stuffed olives, radishes and green pepper.
3 Toss the salad in the French dressing and serve on a bed of lettuce.

Waldorf salad

You will need for 4 servings:
METRIC/IMPERIAL

450 g/1 lb dessert apples, cored and finely chopped	75 g/3 oz walnuts, finely chopped
4 celery stalks, finely chopped	175 ml/6 fl oz mayonnaise
100 g/4 oz seedless raisins	*to serve:* lettuce

1 Mix apples, celery, raisins and walnuts in a large salad bowl.
2 Spoon mayonnaise over ingredients and combine thoroughly.
3 Serve on a bed of lettuce.

Mixed Chinese salad

You will need for 4 servings:
METRIC/IMPERIAL

225 g/8 oz fresh bean sprouts	5-cm/2-inch length cucumber
1 small pineapple, about 175 g/6 oz fruit	5 tablespoons French dressing (see page 86)
50 g/2 oz button mushrooms	1 teaspoon soy sauce
50 g/2 oz radishes	*to garnish:*
100 g/4 oz carrots	watercress

1 Wash the bean sprouts well and place in a bowl.
2 Cut off the ends and skin from the pineapple, remove the coarse centre core, dice the flesh and add to the bean sprouts.
3 Wash and slice the mushrooms and radishes and add to the bowl.
4 Scrape the carrots and cut into matchstick lengths and add.
5 Dice the cucumber and add to the salad.
6 Mix the French dressing and soy sauce together and pour over the salad.
7 Arrange in a serving dish, garnish with the watercress and chill before serving.

Variations:
1 Toast or fry some sesame seeds and sprinkle over the salad.
2 Shred Chinese leaves finely and use instead of bean sprouts.

Green salad

You will need for 6 servings:
METRIC/IMPERIAL

1 crisp lettuce	1 tablespoon chopped
1 small green pepper	parsley
½ cucumber	French dressing (see
1 small onion	page 86)

1 Discard any coarse outside leaves and wash remainder of lettuce. Drain thoroughly.
2 Remove stalk, seeds and white pith from the pepper; cut pepper into thin rings.
3 Peel cucumber, if liked, and cut into thin slices.
4 Prepare and thinly slice the onion.
5 Place these four ingredients in a bowl, sprinkle with parsley, cover and chill until required.
6 Pour dressing over salad just before serving.

Variations:
1 Omit onion and use celery or sliced spring onions.
2 Add watercress, washed and sprigged.
3 Sprinkle cress over the top.
4 Use finely shredded cabbage or Chinese cabbage leaves when lettuce is expensive.

Rice salad bowl

You will need for 6-8 servings:
METRIC/IMPERIAL

225 g/8 oz sliced green beans	½ unpeeled cucumber, sliced
1 bunch radishes, thinly sliced	2 onions, thinly sliced
3 sticks celery, thinly sliced	1 small green pepper, thinly sliced
1 bunch watercress, chopped	300 ml/½ pint mayonnaise (see
675 g/1½ lb cold, cooked long-grain rice, coloured with saffron or yellow colouring	page 87) soy sauce to taste

1 Chill all vegetables and rice.
2 Layer into a glass salad bowl in order given.
3 Blend the mayonnaise with soy sauce to taste, mix well and pour over the salad.
4 Serve well chilled, with any cold meats or hard-boiled eggs.

Indian salad

You will need for 2-3 servings:
METRIC/IMPERIAL

100 g/4 oz long-grain rice	3 tablespoons mayonnaise (see page 87)
100 g/4 oz French beans	1-2 teaspoons concentrated curry sauce
50 g/2 oz button mushrooms, sliced	
5-cm/2-inch length cucumber, diced	

1 Cook the rice in boiling salted water for 15-20 minutes. Rinse in cold water.
2 Cut the beans into 2.5-cm/1-inch lengths and blanch in boiling salted water for 2 minutes. Refresh in cold water.
3 Mix together the rice, beans, mushrooms and cucumber.
4 Blend the mayonnaise with the curry sauce, add to the rice and mix to coat evenly.

Vegetable mould

You will need for 4 servings:
METRIC/IMPERIAL

75 g/3 oz cooked beetroot	to garnish: slices of cucumber
75 g/3 oz cucumber, peeled	radish roses
75 g/3 oz cooked potatoes	for the sauce:
1 stick celery	1 (142-ml/5-fl oz) carton soured cream
2 spring onions	
2 tomatoes	1 tablespoon chopped mixed fresh herbs
1½ teaspoons gelatine	
300 ml/½ pint chicken stock	1 garlic clove, crushed

1 Dice the beetroot, cucumber and potatoes.
2 Slice the celery and spring onions.
3 Peel and chop the tomatoes.
4 Arrange the vegetables in layers, beginning with the beetroot, in a 600 ml/1 pint mould.
5 Dissolve the gelatine in the hot stock over a saucepan of hot water then carefully pour it over the vegetables in the mould.
6 Leave in a cool place until set. Turn out and garnish with slices of cucumber and radish roses.
7 To make the sauce, mix the soured cream, herbs and garlic together. Season and serve with the mould.

Fruit salads
Tossed melon salad

You will need for 4-6 servings:
METRIC/IMPERIAL

1 small melon	100 g/4 oz black grapes
small bunch radishes	Lemon-flavoured French dressing (see page 86)
1 stick celery	
1 small banana	
1 small red apple	2 tablespoons chopped parsley
½ green pepper	

1 Halve and quarter the melon, remove the seeds and cut the flesh into dice, removing from the skin. Place in a bowl.
2 Wash radishes, slice and add to the melon.
3 Wash and slice celery; slice banana and apple. Add to the melon.
4 Wash pepper and remove stalk, seeds and white pith. Cut flesh into slices.
5 Halve grapes and remove seeds.
6 Add the grapes and pepper to the salad.
7 Pour the dressing over the salad.
8 Toss lightly and sprinkle with chopped parsley.
9 Serve with cold cooked bacon.

Red berry salad

You will need for 6-8 servings:
METRIC/IMPERIAL

100 g/4 oz castor sugar	225 g/8 oz strawberries
300 ml/½ pint water	225 g/8 oz raspberries
little egg white	225 g/8 oz redcurrants
225 g/8 oz red cherries	

1 Place the sugar and water in a saucepan and heat slowly to dissolve the sugar. When dissolved, boil gently for 5 minutes. Allow to cool.
2 Brush the rim of a glass serving dish with egg white.
3 Place some castor sugar on a plate and turn the rim of the dish in this so that it looks frosted.
4 Cut the cherries in half, remove stones and place fruit in the dish.
5 Hull the strawberries and halve if necessary.
6 Prepare raspberries and string the redcurrants.
7 Add these to the dish and stir gently to mix the fruits.
8 Pour the cooled syrup over the fruit.
9 Chill well before serving.

Gingered orange and grapefruit

You will need for 4 servings:
METRIC/IMPERIAL

1 large grapefruit	40 g/1½ oz soft brown sugar
2 large oranges	
2 pieces preserved stem ginger, finely chopped	

1 Using a sharp knife, cut off rind and pith from the grapefruit and oranges; cut out the segments from between the membrane. Cut each segment in half.
2 Place these in a serving bowl with the ginger.
3 Sprinkle over the sugar and leave in a cold place.
4 Serve well chilled as a starter or as a fruit salad.

Caramel fruit salad

You will need for 6 servings:

METRIC/IMPERIAL

1 small pineapple	*for the caramel:*
2 ripe pears	75 g/3 oz castor sugar
2 bananas	3 tablespoons water
juice of 1 lemon	
25 g/1 oz Brazil nuts or	
hazelnuts	

1 Prepare the pineapple by trimming off the top and bottom. Cut off the skin, removing all the tough pieces.
2 Cut the pineapple in slices and remove the core from each.
3 Cut the flesh into small segments. Place in an oven-proof glass dish.
4 Peel the pears and cut into dice.
5 Peel and slice the bananas.
6 Add these to the pineapple with the lemon juice; stir so the fruit is coated in lemon. This will help to prevent discolouration.
7 Chop the nuts coarsely and add.
8 To make the caramel, place the sugar and water in a saucepan.
9 Heat gently to dissolve the sugar without boiling.
10 When dissolved, bring to the boil and cook until a rich golden caramel.
11 Pour over the fruit immediately and serve within the hour, otherwise the crunchy caramel will dissolve.

Orange and banana salad

You will need for 4 servings:

METRIC/IMPERIAL

3 oranges	2 tablespoons clear
3 bananas	honey
1 (150-g/5.3-oz)	50 g/2 oz flaked
carton natural	almonds, toasted
yoghurt	

1 Grate the rind from one of the oranges. Remove all the rind and pith from all three oranges and slice, removing the pips.
2 Peel the bananas and slice. Arrange the fruit in a serving dish.
3 Mix the yoghurt with the grated orange rind and honey, then pour over the fruit. Sprinkle the toasted flaked almonds over and serve.
Variation:
For a special dish, add 1 tablespoon of an orange liqueur to the yoghurt dressing before pouring over the fruit.

Pear and grape compôte

You will need for 4 servings:

METRIC/IMPERIAL

100 g/4 oz sugar	4 large firm pears
300 ml/½ pint water	225 g/8 oz black
juice of 1 lemon	grapes
6 tablespoons ginger	
wine	

1 Dissolve the sugar in the water over a low heat. Add the lemon juice and ginger wine and bring to the boil.
2 Peel, core and slice the pears. Add to the syrup and cook gently until just soft.
3 Remove the skin and pips from the grapes before adding to the pears.
4 Chill and serve with whipped cream.
Variation:
For a jellied dessert, add 3 teaspoons gelatine to the liquid and stir until dissolved. Arrange in a suitable mould and chill until set.

Sauces and Dressings

Basic white coating sauce for vegetables

You will need for 300 ml/½ pint:

METRIC/IMPERIAL
25 g/1 oz butter or margarine
25 g/1 oz plain flour

300 ml/½ pint milk (or half vegetable stock and half milk)
seasoning

1 Melt butter or margarine in a saucepan over moderate heat.
2 Remove from the heat and stir in the flour. Cook very slowly for 1-2 minutes.
3 Remove pan from the heat and gradually stir in the milk or stock.
4 Bring to the boil, stirring all the time. Reduce heat and simmer for 2-3 minutes.
5 Add seasoning to taste.

Variations:
1 Parsley: Stir in 1-2 tablespoons chopped parsley.
2 Parsley and egg: Add 1 tablespoon chopped parsley and 1 chopped hard-boiled egg.
3 Onion: Add 2 large chopped and boiled onions at the end.
4 Cheese: Add 50-100 g/2-4 oz grated cheese and a little dry mustard. A little grated onion and crushed garlic also add extra flavour and should be cooked with the butter.
5 Egg: Add 1-2 chopped hard-boiled eggs.
6 Béchamel: Before making the sauce infuse the milk with a piece of onion, carrot, celery, bay leaf and peppercorns. Strain well and follow basic white sauce recipe.

Béarnaise sauce

You will need for 200 ml/8 fl oz:

METRIC/IMPERIAL
2 tablespoons red wine vinegar
1½ teaspoons chopped spring onion
1½ teaspoons chopped fresh tarragon
¼ teaspoon freshly ground black pepper

4 egg yolks
175 g/6 oz softened butter
1 tablespoon fresh parsley, chopped

1 In the top of a double boiler, place the vinegar, onion, tarragon and black pepper.
2 Place on a high heat and reduce to 1 tablespoon of vinegar.
3 Fill the double boiler base with hot, not boiling, water and put on the top of the cooker.
4 Add the egg yolks; whisk with a balloon whisk until just beginning to thicken.

5 Add the butter a tablespoon at a time, whisking each time until melted. The mixture should begin to thicken. Add the parsley.
6 Serve with asparagus or artichokes.

Note:
1 The water should not be too hot as the egg yolks will cook and harden before the necessary emulsion is made.
2 If the water becomes too hot the butter will become oily and cause the sauce to separate.
3 If the sauce separates, start again with an egg yolk and gradually beat in the sauce.

Hollandaise sauce

You will need for 4-6 servings:

METRIC/IMPERIAL
2 tablespoons water
2 teaspoons white wine vinegar
6 peppercorns
blade of mace

175 g/6 oz unsalted butter
2 large egg yolks
seasoning
lemon juice

1 Place the water, vinegar, peppercorns and mace in a small saucepan.
2 Heat gently and reduce to 1 tablespoon; strain and allow to cool.
3 Meanwhile, place the butter in a small saucepan, heat gently to just melt, do not allow it to become oily.
4 Place the egg yolks, the reduced vinegar and a little salt in a small bowl over a pan of cold water. Heat very gently, whisking the egg yolks until they are thick and pale in colour. Remove bowl from the heat, gradually whisk in the melted butter. Add extra salt and pepper and a little lemon juice if a sharper flavour is required.

Note:
If the butter is used too hot it will begin to cook the egg yolks and therefore will affect the bulk and consistency of the sauce.

Piquant tomato and olive sauce

You will need for 4 servings:

METRIC/IMPERIAL
1 tablespoon oil
1 medium onion, chopped
450 g/1 lb fresh tomatoes, skinned and chopped
2 tablespoons vinegar

1 tablespoon granulated sugar
1 teaspoon Worcestershire sauce
75 g/3 oz stuffed olives, chopped

1 Heat the oil in a saucepan with the onion and cook without browning about 5 minutes.
2 Add the tomatoes and cook down to a pulp, about 5 minutes.
3 Stir in the remaining ingredients. Heat through and serve with pasta.

Sauce italienne

You will need for 4-5 servings:

METRIC/IMPERIAL

1 tablespoon olive oil	3 tablespoons dry
1 onion, chopped	white wine
1 small green pepper,	1 tablespoon tomato
seeded and cut into	purée
dice	2 teaspoons castor
2 cloves garlic,	sugar
crushed	2 teaspoons dried
1 (397-g/14-oz) can	marjoram
peeled tomatoes	seasoning

1 Place the oil in a saucepan with the onion and cook for 5 minutes without browning.
2 Add the pepper, garlic, tomatoes and wine.
3 Cover and boil for 15 minutes; remove lid and continue boiling fairly briskly for 15 minutes to reduce to a thick pulp.
4 Stir in remaining ingredients.
5 Serve with aubergines or pasta.

Pepperoni sauce

You will need for 4-5 servings:

METRIC/IMPERIAL

3 tablespoons olive oil	300 ml/½ pint stock
25 g/1 oz butter	50 g/2 oz button
1 large onion, sliced	mushrooms,
1 medium-sized	washed and thinly
carrot, cut into thin	sliced
strips	1 teaspoon
1 medium-sized red	granulated sugar
pepper, sliced	seasoning
3 tablespoons flour	
150 ml/¼ pint dry	
white wine	

1 Place the oil and butter in a saucepan with the onion, carrot and pepper.
2 Cook until soft without browning, about 8 minutes.
3 Stir in the flour and cook for 2 minutes, add the wine, stirring all the time, and cook for a few minutes.
4 Gradually add the stock and bring to the boil. Cook for 3 minutes.
5 Stir in the remaining ingredients and cook for 2 minutes.
6 Serve with chicken or pasta.

Country vegetable sauce

You will need for 4 servings:

METRIC/IMPERIAL

40 g/1½ oz butter or	2 tablespooons flour
margarine	1 tablespoon dry
1 medium onion,	sherry
finely chopped	300 ml/½ pint stock
1 tablespoon castor	½-1 teaspoon dried
sugar	mixed herbs to taste
1 small turnip, finely	1 tablespoon chopped
diced	fresh parsley
2 small carrots, thinly	seasoning
sliced	
1 stick celery, thinly	
sliced	

1 Melt the butter, add the onion and sugar, cook gently for 5 minutes.
2 Add the turnip, carrots and celery and stir. Cover with a piece of damp greaseproof paper, then cover with the lid and cook gently for 10 minutes until the vegetables are just tender.
3 Stir in the flour and cook for 1 minute.
4 Add the sherry and gradually stir in the stock. Bring to the boil and cook for 2 minutes.
5 Add the remaining ingredients.
6 Serve with chicken, lamb or bacon joints.

Basic French dressing

You will need for 4 servings:

METRIC/IMPERIAL

½ teaspoon salt	3 tablespoons salad
⅛ level teaspoon	oil
pepper	1½ tablespoons white
½ level teaspoon	wine vinegar
French mustard	
½ level teaspoon	
castor sugar	

1 Place the seasonings and sugar in a screw-top jar.
2 Add the oil and vinegar and replace the lid.
3 Shake well and serve.
Variations:
1 Add a clove of garlic to the jar.
2 Use other types of vinegar.

Lemon-flavoured French dressing

You will need for 4 servings:

METRIC/IMPERIAL

seasoning	4 tablespoons olive oil
1 teaspoon castor	1 tablespoon wine
sugar	vinegar
1 shallot, finely	2 teaspoons lemon
chopped	juice

1 Place the seasoning, sugar and shallot in a screw-top jar.
2 Add the oil, vinegar, lemon juice, shake well and use as required.

Mint vinaigrette

You will need for 3 tablespoons:

METRIC/IMPERIAL

pinch each salt,
  pepper, dry
  mustard and castor
  sugar
2 tablespoons corn oil

1 tablespoon cider
  vinegar
2 tablespoons freshly
  chopped mint

1 Place the seasonings in a screw-top jar.
2 Add the oil, vinegar and mint; shake well before using.
3 Use in French style pea salad (see page 80) or over new boiled potatoes.

Mayonnaise

You will need for 300 ml/½ pint:

METRIC/IMPERIAL

¼ teaspoon salt
¼ teaspoon pepper
¼ teaspoon dry
  mustard
2 egg yolks
300 ml/½ pint corn oil

1 teaspoon boiling
  water
1½ teaspoons vinegar
  – white wine, red
  wine, tarragon or
  cider

1 Place the seasonings and egg yolks in a bowl. Place bowl on a damp cloth to steady it.
2 Blend in the seasonings with a wooden spoon.
3 Add the oil drop by drop, beating well each time until the mixture is thick.
4 After adding about 2 tablespoons of oil, beat in the boiling water gradually.
5 The oil can now be added a tablespoon at a time.
6 Beat in half of the selected vinegar.
7 Gradually add the remaining oil and the remaining vinegar if necessary.
8 This sauce is now ready for serving. Taste and add extra salt if necessary.
Notes:
1 The eggs should be a standard size. Large eggs would give too strong an egg flavour.
2 The boiling water is a trick of mine and makes mayonnaise making easier and gives a lighter result.
Variations:
1 Add grated lemon rind and chopped parsley.
2 Add a selection of freshly chopped herbs.
3 Add chopped stuffed olives and chopped parsley.
4 Tartare sauce: Add chopped capers, gherkins, parsley and a little grated onion.
5 Orange mayonnaise: Add grated orange rind and a little juice.
6 Curry-flavoured mayonnaise: Add concentrated curry sauce and a teaspoon of lemon juice to the egg yolks.
7 Tomato mayonnaise: Add concentrated tomato purée and a little sugar to the egg yolks.
8 Chopped dill, fennel, chervil or tarragon make a very special mayonnaise to serve with fish.

Sour cream and mayonnaise dressing

You will need for 6-8 servings:

METRIC/IMPERIAL

3 tablespoons
  mayonnaise (see
  above)
3 tablespoons natural
  yoghurt

2 tablespoons soured
  cream
seasoning

1 Place all the ingredients in a small bowl and blend together.
2 Serve with new potatoes or as a dressing over tomatoes, beetroot or tossed in a salad.
Variations:
1 Add chopped parsley, fennel or chopped fresh chives.
2 Add to cream cheese with crispy fried bacon, crumbled, and use as a dip to serve with fingers of carrot, celery, cauliflower and fennel.

Curried mayonnaise

You will need for 4 servings:

METRIC/IMPERIAL

pinch each salt and
  pepper
1 teaspoon curry
  paste
1 teaspoon castor
  sugar

1 egg yolk
200 ml/8 fl oz corn oil
2 teaspoons white
  wine vinegar

1 Place the seasonings in a bowl with the curry paste, sugar and egg yolk.
2 Blend well together and gradually add the oil drop by drop until about half has been added.
3 Add 1 teaspoon of vinegar and gradually add remaining oil and vinegar a little faster until all is thoroughly blended.
4 Serve as required.

Thousand Island Dressing

You will need for 300 ml/½ pint:

METRIC/IMPERIAL

150 ml/¼ pint
  mayonnaise (see
  page 87)
2 tablespoons tomato
  ketchup
50 g/2 oz pimiento-
  stuffed olives
50 g/2 oz piece of
  green pepper

2 large spring onions,
  trimmed to the
  white part
1 hard-boiled egg,
  shelled
2 teaspoons chopped
  fresh parsley

1 Place the mayonnaise and ketchup in a bowl. Stir.
2 Mince the olives, green pepper, spring onion and egg into the bowl, stir and add the parsley.

3 Serve as a dip with crudités or over cold chicken. Serve spooned over cold cooked broccoli as a starter.

Variations:

1 Use chopped chives instead of spring onions.

2 If a hotter sauce is preferred, use 2 tablespoons of chilli sauce.

Blue cheese sauce

You will need for 4-6 servings:

METRIC/IMPERIAL

50 g/2 oz Danish blue cheese
1 (142-ml/5-fl oz) carton soured cream
pinch castor sugar
pinch dry mustard
½-1 teaspoon grated onion

1 tablespoon oil
2 teaspoons lemon juice
1 tablespoon chopped parsley
freshly ground pepper

1 Grate the Danish blue cheese. Place in a bowl with the soured cream.

2 Place the seasonings and onion in a bowl, blend in the oil and gradually beat in the lemon juice.

3 Blend this mixture into the soured cream and cheese.

4 Add pepper and parsley and serve with Cauliflower salad (see page 77).

Index